PEOPLE
IN THE NEWS

Michael Jackson

Titles in the People in the News series include:

PEOPLE
IN THE NEWS

Michael Jackson

by Karen Marie Graves

Lucent Books, San Diego, CA

Library of Congress Cataloging-in-Publication Data

Graves, Karen Marie
    Michael Jackson / by Karen M. Graves.
        p. cm. — (People in the news)
    Includes bibliographical references and index.
    Summary: A biography of the pop star and performer known as much for his eccentricities and plastic surgeries as for his music and talent.
    ISBN 1-56006-707-1 (hardcover)
    1. Jackson, Michael, 1958—Juvenile literature. 2. Rock musicians—United States—Biography—Juvenile literature. [1. Jackson, Michael, 1958– 2. Entertainers. 3. Afro-Americans—Biography.] I. Title. II. People in the news   (San Diego, Calif.)
    ML3930.J25 G73   2001
    782.42166'092—dc21

                                                            00–008929

JB
JACKSON, M,

c. 4

Copyright © 2001 by Lucent Books, Inc.
P.O. Box 289011
San Diego, CA 92198-9011
Printed in the U.S.A.

Table of Contents

Foreword

FAME AND CELEBRITY are alluring. People are drawn to those who walk in fame's spotlight, whether they are known for great accomplishments or for notorious deeds. The lives of the famous pique public interest and attract attention, perhaps because their experiences seem in some ways so different from, yet in other ways so similar to, our own.

Newspapers, magazines, and television regularly capitalize on this fascination with celebrity by running profiles of famous people. For example, television programs such as *Entertainment Tonight* devote all of their programming to stories about entertainment and entertainers. Magazines such as *People* fill their pages with stories of the private lives of famous people. Even newspapers, newsmagazines, and television news frequently delve into the lives of well-known personalities. Despite the number of articles and programs, few provide more than a superficial glimpse at their subjects.

Lucent's People in the News series offers young readers a deeper look into the lives of today's newsmakers, the influences that have shaped them, and the impact they have had in their fields of endeavor and on other people's lives. The subjects of the series hail from many disciplines and walks of life. They include authors, musicians, athletes, political leaders, entertainers, entrepreneurs, and others who have made a mark on modern life and who, in many cases, will continue to do so for years to come.

These biographies are more than factual chronicles. Each book emphasizes the contributions, accomplishments, or deeds that have brought fame or notoriety to the individual and shows how that person has influenced modern life. Authors portray their subjects in a realistic, unsentimental light. For example, Bill Gates—the cofounder and chief executive officer of the software giant Microsoft—has been instrumental in making personal computers the most vital tool of the modern age. Few dispute his business savvy, his perseverance, or his technical expertise, yet critics say he is ruthless in his dealings with competitors and driven more by his desire to maintain Microsoft's dominance in the computer industry than by an interest in furthering technology.

In these books, young readers will encounter inspiring stories about real people who achieved success despite enormous obstacles. Oprah Winfrey—the most powerful, most watched, and wealthiest woman on television today—spent the first six years of her life in the care of her grandparents while her unwed mother sought work and a better life elsewhere. Her adolescence was colored by promiscuity, pregnancy at age fourteen, rape, and sexual abuse.

Each author documents and supports his or her work with an array of primary and secondary source quotations taken from diaries, letters, speeches, and interviews. All quotes are footnoted to show readers exactly how and where biographers derive their information and provide guidance for further research. The quotations enliven the text by giving readers eyewitness views of the life and accomplishments of each person covered in the People in the News series.

In addition, each book in the series includes photographs, annotated bibliographies, timelines, and comprehensive indexes. For both the casual reader and the student researcher, the People in the News series offers insight into the lives of today's newsmakers—people who shape the way we live, work, and play in the modern age.

Introduction

Entertainer of the '80s

"I'M GONNA MAKE you the biggest thing in the world, and you're gonna be written about in history books."[1] So said Berry Gordy Jr., founder of Motown Records, to the Jackson Five soon after they had passed the audition for Motown in 1968. He was right—at least about the group's extraordinarily gifted youngest member, Michael. Michael Jackson went on to make *Thriller*, the biggest-selling album of all time, and he has broken just about every existing record pertaining to popular music. It's no wonder Michael Jackson is known as "the King of Pop."

As the twentieth century drew to a close and the twenty-first began, there were innumerable retrospectives, awards, and lists recognizing and honoring the greatest artists and works of the last one hundred years. In virtually every one, whether compiled by professionals or voted on by fans, Michael Jackson came out on top. He was voted Male Entertainer of 1900–2000 by the on-line readers of *Entertainment Weekly;* the CNN on-line "Millennium Poll" ranked him as the number-one artist, beating out Leonardo da Vinci, Pablo Picasso, Ludwig van Beethoven, and Vincent van Gogh; he was recognized as the Artist of the '80s at the twenty-seventh annual American Music Awards; and he was selected the artist or entertainer of the 1980s in poll after poll. *Thriller* was number one in MTV's "Top 100 Greatest Videos Ever Made," and it was chosen by the editors of *TV Guide* and MTV producers and executives as one of the hundred best videos ever made and the number-two video of the century—behind the video of Martin Luther King Jr.'s "I Have a Dream" speech. *Thriller* was also named the number-one music video by Black Entertainment Television.

8

Michael Jackson's music and talent have made him one of the world's most popular entertainers.

An enormously talented performer who has described himself as "one of the loneliest people on this earth,"[2] Michael Jackson is a study in what went right and what went wrong in the life of a child star who became extremely popular at an early age. But he is known as much for his insecurities and eccentricities as for his music and talent. Whatever else he is, Michael Jackson is a complex, complicated man.

Chapter 1

Born to Perform

ON THE WARM summer night of August 29, 1958, in the industrial city of Gary, Indiana, Michael Joseph Jackson was born to Katherine and Joseph "Joe" Jackson. The seventh of nine children, he joined sisters Maureen Reilette, "Rebbie," eight, and LaToya Yvonne, two, and brothers Sigmund Esco, "Jackie," seven, Tariano Adaryl, "Tito," four, Jermaine LaJuane, three, and Marlon David, one and a half. Another brother, Steven Randall, "Randy," would be born three years later, and another sister, Janet Dameta, would be born about a year and a half after that.

There was nothing at the time to indicate that Michael would be any different from all of the other kids living in Gary. But before long, his family knew that he was unique. "Ever since Michael was very young, he seemed different to me from the rest of the children," said his mother, Katherine. "I don't know where he got it from. He was just so good, so young. Some kids are special. Michael was special."[3]

Michael was, indeed, special. From an early age he displayed an extraordinary sense of rhythm and movement: At eighteen months, he loved to dance to the sounds of the washing machine. His mother once said, "I don't believe in reincarnation, but you know how babies move uncoordinated? He never moved that way. When he danced, it was like he was an older person."[4] And he soon proved to have a talent for singing as well. At three, according to his grandmother Chrystal Johnson, Michael already had a beautiful voice, and even at that young age he delighted everyone who listened to him.

Jackson Family Talent

Michael was not the first person in his family to display musical talent. His great-great-grandfather Kendall Brown had sung in church and had been renowned for his voice throughout Russell County, Alabama, where the family lived. Michael's mother played clarinet and piano and was a member of her high school's orchestra and choir as well as her church's junior band. And she, like her great-grandfather, had a pure, glorious voice. Because of this, Jackson believes he inherited his singing ability from his mother.

The path to stardom for the Jacksons began when Joe Jackson became aware of his sons' musical abilities.

Michael's father, Joe, a crane operator at a steel mill in East Chicago, also influenced Michael musically. Joe played guitar, and he earned a little extra income by playing in a blues band called the Falcons, which was the fulfillment of his own child-hood dream. Joe had always wanted to perform, so he and his brother started a group. The Falcons played in small clubs and bars in Gary and neighboring Chicago. But it would be Joe Jackson's drive and talent for staging and refining an act and winning over an audience that would propel the entire family—and Michael in particular—into the world of big-time music.

The Jackson Boys' Talent Is Discovered

Given the talents of the elder Jacksons, perhaps it is no surprise that their children showed an interest in music as well. Michael's oldest brothers, Jackie, Tito, and Jermaine, loved to sit in on the Falcons' rehearsals at home and watch their dad play his guitar. It was not long before they had to try out what they had seen and heard. This was in the early 1960s, and as Jackie later recalled:

> Everybody we knew was in a singing group. That was the thing to do, go join a group. There were gangs, and there were singing groups. I wanted to be in a singing group, but we weren't allowed to hang out with the other kids. So we started singing together 'round the house. Our TV broke down and Mother started having us sing together. And then what happened was that our father would go to work, and we would sneak into his bedroom and get that guitar down.[5]

Tito played his father's guitar and Jackie and Jermaine sang.

Joe discovered their secret when, after a few months, Tito broke a string. Angry at his son for playing with his prized possession, Joe gave Tito a beating. But when Tito told him that he could really play, Joe asked him to prove it. What Joe saw and heard when his sons proceeded to play and sing amazed and delighted him.

Faced with his sons' obvious talent, Joe revised his dream. He decided he would leave the music to his sons, and his dream was now for them. They would be the ones onstage performing,

Katherine Scruse Jackson

One of Michael Jackson's first memories is of his mother, Katherine, holding him and singing to him. And she has remained an ever-present influence and inspiration in his life. In *Moonwalk*, his autobiography, Jackson discusses the values she instilled in him:

> The lessons she taught us were invaluable. Kindness, love, and consideration for other people headed her list. Don't hurt people. Never beg. Never freeload. Those were sins at our house. She always wanted us to *give*, but she never wanted us to ask or beg.

Katherine, a devout Jehovah's Witness drew strength from her deep and abiding faith. Katherine was stricken with polio as a toddler, and had to wear a brace or use crutches until she was sixteen. Other children teased her about this and she became shy and introverted. But she later saw the polio and its aftermath as a challenge from God—one over which she triumphed. Katherine passed that faith on to her son.

captivating audiences with their talent—talent he believed they had inherited from him.

So he bought Tito a bright red guitar and made the boys rehearse. He taught them rhythm-and-blues songs, and soon the three boys were practicing three hours a day. Tito recalled that those were happy times for the family: "We'd never been so close. It was as if we had finally found something in common. Marlon and Mike, they would sit in the corner and watch. . . . I noticed our mother and father were happy. We were all happy. We had found something. Something special."[6]

At first Rebbie and LaToya accompanied the three boys on violin and clarinet, but Joe was focused on the boys, and they formed a trio around 1961. As the younger Jacksons grew, they joined in with their older brothers. Marlon joined the group in 1962, when he was five. And Michael, just a year younger, was brought in after he imitated Jermaine singing a James Brown song. The older siblings immediately recognized his talent. With his charisma, energy, and exceptional ability to sing, dance, and mimic, everyone soon agreed that he should be the lead singer in the group. Even Jermaine, whose feelings were hurt because he had been replaced as lead singer, had to agree that Michael's talent was immense. As Jackie remembers:

Michael was so energetic that at five years old he was like a leader. We saw that. So we said, "Hey, Michael, you be the lead guy." The audience ate it up. He was into those James Brown things at the time. The speed was the thing. He would see somebody do something and he could do it right away.[7]

Joe's Control Increases

Joe devoted ever-increasing effort to advancing the boys' career. And more and more he and Katherine disagreed over where the family was headed. The couple would argue about Joe using the family's money to buy musical equipment, instruments, amplifiers, and microphones. But Joe was unrelenting in his arguments, so convinced was he that the boys would be successful. Joe later explained:

You have to understand that I saw this great potential in my sons. So yes, I did go overboard. I invested a lot of money in instruments, and this was money we did not have. . . . She'd yell at me that the money should have been put into food, not into guitars and drums. But I was the head of the household and what I said was the final word.[8]

Joe Jackson's control over his household extended well beyond the family's budget. He made the boys practice every day when they came home from school. And every day he supervised the practice sessions, trying to instill in his sons his own drive for perfection while making certain that they persisted until they performed to his satisfaction.

Such a grueling schedule left little time for fun or friends. Years later, during her interview with Michael Jackson on an ABC television special on February 10, 1993, talk-show host Oprah Winfrey asked how big a price he had paid for this kind of life. Jackson observed: "Well, you don't get to do things that other children get to do, you know, having friends and slumber parties and buddies. There was none of that for me. I didn't have any friends when I was little. My brothers were my friends."[9]

In his drive to develop his sons' talents, Joe Jackson proved to be a hard taskmaster. His own father, Samuel Jackson, had been a strict disciplinarian who ruled with an iron hand and rarely showed affection. Joe used the same approach. He maintains that he does not remember any beatings as being violent, but the children do. In fact, in a special television edition of *People* magazine, Joe called them "little spankings."[10] There is no question, though, that Joe would strike the children when he felt they deserved punishment, and he became more violent as he got older. Sometimes things got out of hand. A family friend recalls one incident:

> One time, Michael was late for rehearsal and when he walked in, Joe came up behind him and pushed him into some musical instruments. Michael fell into the drums and got banged up pretty bad. Maybe Joe didn't mean to shove him so hard, I don't know. But Michael was affected. I know for a fact that Michael began to dislike his father at an early age. Where the other boys could take their father's temper more or less with a grain of salt, Michael was especially sensitive to it.[11]

"If you messed up during rehearsal, you got hit," Michael later said. "Sometimes with a belt. Sometimes with a switch."[12] Because he antagonized his father by fighting back, Michael received more frequent, and more severe beatings than his brothers—especially later, when he became aware of his importance to the group and had a bad attitude at rehearsals.

The boys hated the physical punishments that their father inflicted on them, but they loved making the music he compelled them to practice so diligently. And they loved the dream he had passed on to them. They just wondered when they would have the chance to perform before an audience.

Performing Publicly

Finally, in 1964, when Michael was six, Joe decided that the boys were ready to perform publicly, and the Jacksons entered their first talent contest at Roosevelt High in Gary. They sang the Temptations' "My Girl" and Robert Parker's "Barefootin',"

*From the Jackson Five's first performance, Michael was able to captivate
and entertain an audience with his singing and dancing ability.*

in which during a musical break, to the delight of the audience,
Michael kicked off his shoes and did a barefoot dance all over
the stage. The Jacksons won the contest, and after that, they won
every contest they entered, including Gary's first City-Wide
Talent Show. Calling themselves the Ripples and Waves plus
Michael, they gave their first noncontest performance, a hospital benefit, at a Big Top supermarket in Gary.

A short time after that, the Jacksons performed professionally for the first time at a Gary nightclub named Mr. Lucky's.
Nobody got rich that night: The Jackson Brothers, as Joe had renamed the group, were paid less than ten dollars for the engagement. But at subsequent performances, the boys did better.
Patrons threw coins and bills onto the stage, and Michael
learned to utilize dance steps, executing dips, spins, and splits to
pick up the cash, which motivated the audience to throw even
more. "My pockets would be loaded with money," Michael said.

"We would have around $300 lying on the stage, and we would make just $15 from the manager [of the club] paying us."[13]

While his sons were performing, Joe visited other clubs to check out other groups, and he would come home and report on what he had seen. He would use what he learned to refine the Jackson Brothers' act, planning every detail, from choreography to clothes, shoes, and hairstyles. Perhaps most importantly, Joe taught his sons how to handle and win over an audience. Michael Jackson remembers: "Though he [Joe] had a group, he was never a real showman but he knew exactly what I had to do to become a professional. He taught me exactly how to hold a mike and make gestures to the crowd and how to handle an audience."[14]

Michael's extraordinary ability to mimic what he saw proved to be invaluable from the beginning. He would see a new dance step on television, memorize what he saw, practice it, then show the other boys. Soon he was choreographing the show.

By 1967 the boys had a new name, The Jackson Five, suggested by a family friend, and they were performing on the weekends, sometimes as many as fourteen shows in two days. Despite the fact that they returned home at about 4:00 or 5:00 on Monday morning and had to go to school on only a couple of hours' sleep, their parents insisted that they keep up their studies. The boys knew that they had to maintain their grades or they would be taken off the road, so they often did homework while Joe drove them from one show to the next in their Volkswagen bus. When it got too dark for them to study, Joe talked to them or they sang—sometimes traditional songs they had learned at home and sometimes current rhythm-and-blues hits they were learning. Then they might finally fall asleep for two or three hours. It was exhausting, but Joe believed it was necessary: "I saw the potential in them being big stars. And so we worked toward that goal, and they had to be talked to all the time, with a skillful hand. With an iron hand."[15]

Difficult as life on the road was, the stage was already becoming home for Michael, and performing was already beginning to supersede other parts of his life. He was happy onstage, and he looked happy. Offstage he felt sad, lonely, and out of place. In her nationally televised interview with him, Oprah Winfrey asked Jackson if, as a child, he had been as happy offstage as he had appeared onstage. He explained his feelings of sadness and isolation:

> Well, on stage for me was home. I was most comfortable on stage but once I got off stage, I was like, very sad. . . . Lonely, sad, having to face popularity and all that. There were times when I had great times with my brothers, pillow fights and things, but I was, used to always cry from loneliness.[16]

By 1966 the Jackson Five had begun to produce enough income that Joe could take on the job of managing them full time and cut back to working part time at the steel mill. Joe was certain that the group would make a lot of money, and that he was the best—indeed, the only—manager for his boys. Michael later acknowledged his father's hard work and good intentions as their manager:

> My father did always protect us and that's no small feat. He always tried to make sure people didn't cheat us. He looked after our interests in the best ways. He might have made a few mistakes along the way, but he always thought he was doing what was right for the family.[17]

What Joe thought was right for his boys at that time was to get as much experience and exposure as they could, wherever they could. He felt that they could not afford to be picky about performance venues that included strip joints, which displeased Katherine, who was a devout Jehovah's Witness.

Learning from the Best

When Michael was eight, Joe Jackson decided that his sons were ready for what was known as "the chitlin' circuit": clubs and theaters in urban African American neighborhoods. In these large theaters, located in downtown areas of large cities such as Philadelphia, Cleveland, and Washington, D.C., established artists and unknowns played on the same bill, affording the newer performers the opportunity to learn from the more expe-

Michael Jackson's mother Katherine (left), and sister Janet. Jackson feels that his mother's guidance has profoundly influenced his life.

rienced ones. Michael's talent for mimicry made this type of exposure invaluable to him.

After the Jackson Five performed, Michael always stayed in the wings and studied the other acts, watching and learning from the best. James Brown, nicknamed "the Godfather of Soul," and Jackie Wilson were two of his idols, and he would watch them over and over again. Then he would practice the techniques and steps he had seen and show his brothers how to incorporate them into their act.

The Jackson Five were gaining experience and polishing their act, and onstage Michael was becoming more professional and self-assured. The group played Kansas City, St. Louis, Boston,

Born to Perform

Michael Jackson believes that he was born to perform and entertain
and that it was his talent—not his father's demands—that drove him
to succeed.

> I remember my childhood as mostly work, even though I *loved*
> to sing. I wasn't *forced* into this business by stage parents the
> way Judy Garland was. I did it because I enjoyed it and because
> it was as natural to me as drawing a breath and exhaling it. I
> did it because I was *compelled* to do it, not by parents or fam-
> ily, but by my own inner life in the world of music.

Milwaukee, and Philadelphia and opened for big-name per-
formers such as the Temptations, the O'Jays, the Emotions,
Jackie Wilson, Sam and Dave, and Bobby Taylor and the
Vancouvers.

The Apollo

Finally, in the summer of 1967, came a breakthrough. The
Jackson Five performed at amateur night at the famous Apollo
Theater in Harlem. It was difficult—and an honor—just to be
invited to appear. This was the proving ground for black entertainers at the time, and the audience was tough. Jackson remembered that he and his brothers maintained their confidence
despite the pressure:

> That was the toughest place of all to play, the Apollo
> Theater. If they liked you there, they really *liked* you.
> And if they hated you, they'd throw things at you, food
> and stuff. But we weren't scared. We knew we were
> good. At the other gigs we'd played, we had -em in the
> palms of our hands, you know? I'd be on stage singing
> and I'd look over at Jermaine and we'd wink at one an-
> other. We always knew we had it.[18]

And have it they did. The Jackson Five won amateur night and
received a standing ovation. They were on their way.

With this victory, the Jackson Five got their first taste of the perks
and power of stardom. Michael was enthralled by the attention:

At the Apollo, girls bought stuff for us. . . . You know, watches and rings and things. And we didn't even tell them to do it. We didn't even know they were coming. I mean, we didn't even know them and they were giving us watches.[19]

The brothers' celebrity was enhanced back home when they signed with a local label, Steeltown Records. They released a couple of mediocre singles, but promotion and distribution of the recordings were poor. And though the boys were initially excited, feeling certain they had finally made it, they still wanted more. Little did they know how much more was to come.

Chapter 2

Michael and Motown

In May 1968 the Jacksons were invited to play the Apollo again, and this time they were paid for their performance. But that was just the first step in the realization of the family dream. They played the Regal in Chicago later that year, and Gladys Knight, the popular lead singer of Gladys Knight and the Pips, arranged for some executives from Motown Records—the premier label for black music—to attend the show. Then, in July, the Jacksons were the opening act for Bobby Taylor and the Vancouvers at the High Chaparral Club in Chicago, and Taylor recommended that the Jacksons be allowed to audition for Motown. Raynard Miner, one of the producers at Motown, knew the group's reputation and agreed to film an audition to send to Berry Gordy Jr., founder of Motown Records, who was in Los Angeles.

The group was scheduled to leave for New York when their engagement at the High Chaparral Club was finished. After their sensational performance at the Apollo, the Jacksons had been invited to perform on *The David Frost Show*, a nationally syndicated television show filmed in New York. But when the boys learned that Joe had canceled their trip to New York because they had been invited to audition on film for Motown, they were elated. This was the chance for which they had been hoping and waiting.

Michael Jackson felt certain that, once given that chance, he and his brothers would amaze everyone. He remembered feeling excited and confident: "When we tore it down at the Apollo, we finally felt that nothing could stand in our way. We were going to Motown, and nothing there was going to surprise us either. We were going to surprise them, just like we always did."[20]

Motown at Last

Michael was right. When Berry Gordy saw the audition film, he made an instantaneous decision to sign the Jacksons. He believed they would be a hit, and he told them so. Jackson later recalled what it was like to hear Berry Gordy's predictions:

> I remember Berry Gordy sitting us all down and saying that we were going to make history together. . . . I'll never forget that. We were all over at his house, and it was like a fairy tale come true listening to this powerful, talented man tell us we were going to be very big. Your first record will be a number one, your second record will be a number one, and so will your third record.[21]

Gordy knew what he was talking about. Motown was one of the largest black-owned companies in the world, for good reason. Gordy had a unique ability to recognize and develop talent. He knew the music business, and he knew what the public liked and wanted. Gordy had created the original, very infectious, popular style of music known as the Motown Sound. He also controlled every aspect of the company, including the performers.

Gordy hired professional dance, music, and etiquette instructors to train his young artists through the artist development

Learning from a Pro

When Michael and his brothers were invited back to the Apollo, they were on a bill with Etta James, a popular rhythm-and-blues singer. True to form, Michael studied James so intently from the wings that she finally told him to scat. Later, according to J. Randy Taraborrelli in *Michael Jackson: The Magic and the Madness*, Michael went to James's dressing room to apologize: "Miss James," Michael implored, "I'm sorry ma'am, but I was just watchin' you 'cause you're so good. I mean, you're just so *good*. How do you do that? How do you make them want more? I never seen people clap like that." She was flattered and invited him in to teach him a few tricks. Young Michael had made quite an impression on Etta James. She later recalled, "I remember him being talented, yes. But polite and interested too. I remember thinking as he was leaving, 'Now there's a boy who wants to learn from the best, so one day he's gonna be the best.'"

division of Motown. This preparation was an important contributing factor to the success of his stars. Michael and his brothers were taught how to sing, dance, dress, act, and talk. Jackson recalled how they were coached and prepared for interviews and questions from the media: "We had classes in manners and grammar. They gave us a list of questions, and they said they were the kinds of questions that we could expect people to ask us. . . . The Motown people tested us on the answers to questions we hadn't heard from anyone yet. They tested us on grammar."[22]

One of the areas over which Gordy exerted the most influence was image. He created and perpetuated the image of the Jacksons as the ideal close, loving family. And he subtracted two years from the ages of the boys to make them seem even younger, and therefore more talented, than they were. Another frequently repeated Motown myth was that Diana Ross, the label's reigning superstar, had discovered the Jackson Five in September 1968 at a benefit concert in Gary to raise funds for Richard Hatcher's mayoral campaign. In fact, Motown had booked that concert, but Ross did not actually meet the Jackson Five until they performed in December of that year at a party for big-name Motown artists at Gordy's Detroit estate.

In the following exchange with Pauline Dunn, a reporter from the *Sentinel,* an African American newspaper in Los Angeles, a young Michael demonstrates what the Jacksons were taught and how quickly he learned:

"How's it feel to be a star?" she wanted to know.

"Well, to tell you the truth, I had just about given up hope," Michael said with a grin. He was wearing a black British bowler over his Afro-style hair. "I thought I was gonna be an old man before being discovered." Then, in a hushed, dramatic tone he concluded, "But then along came Miss Diana Ross to save my career. She *discovered* me."

"And just how old are you, Michael?" she asked.

"Eight," Michael said quickly.

"But I thought you were older. Going on eleven, maybe," the suspicious journalist pressed.

"Well, I'm not," Michael insisted. "I'm eight."

"But I heard—"

"Look, the kid's eight, all right?" Gordy broke in. "Next question."[23]

Michael learned early and well how Motown fed the public lies to create an image. In fact, he felt that he had to educate his older brothers about it. He later explained: "I figured out at an early age that if someone said something about me that wasn't

Berry Gordy Jr., the founder of Motown Records and the man who orchestrated the Jackson Five's rise to fame.

true, it was a lie. But if someone said something about my *image* that wasn't true, then it was okay. Because then it wasn't a lie, it was public relations."[24]

It was obvious to any observer that Michael was a quick study—in the promotion and public relations as well as the creative and performing aspects of the business. But it was not just the concepts and techniques that he absorbed, he assimilated the images he helped create. Stan Sherman, a promotion man, perceived what he believed could become a problem later for Michael:

> He was really into this image thing at a pretty early age. The other boys were sort of befuddled about all the lies. But not Michael. Once you explained it to him, he not only agreed with it, but I think, he even started to believe it. That was, to me, just a bit frightening. He seemed a little too eager to adjust to the fantasy of it all.[25]

Berry Gordy Jr.'s Influence

Gordy shaped more than Michael's interview responses and his image. He also helped shape the boy's outlook and attitude toward work and the music industry. Jackson acknowledged Gordy's influence when recalling the long recording session (until two in the morning) for "I Want You Back," the Jacksons' first record for Motown:

> That's the way Motown did things in those days because Berry insisted on perfection and attention to detail. I'll never forget his persistence. This was his genius. Then and later, I observed every moment of the sessions where Berry was present and never forgot what I learned. To this day I use the same principles. Berry was my teacher and a great one. He could identify the little elements that would make a song *great* rather than just good.[26]

Gordy used "the Corporation," a talented team headed by Deke Richards, with Freddy Perrin, "Fonce" Mizell, Bobby Taylor, and Hal Davis, to write and produce the Jacksons' early records. Gordy also remained involved in the writing and pro-

The Jackson Five pose for a newspaper photo in 1970. Front row (left to right), Marlon and Michael. Back row (left to right), Tito, Jackie, and Jermaine.

ducing. The team worked with the group as they recorded a song, changing and refining it until it was perfect. They would cut a track over and over, sometimes for weeks, until it was exactly how the Corporation wanted it. Michael watched and learned from them as they changed everything—words, arrangements, and rhythms—and kept improving it. A perfectionist himself, Gordy allowed the Corporation the control, freedom, and time required to make everything just right.

Michael's brothers also recognized Gordy's brilliance and perfectionism, but they did not emulate him, or his principles, as Michael did. Instead, they seemed to view Gordy's ever-present control and influence as an inconvenience and the process as grueling. As Jermaine later recalled: "This is when I began to understand the Motown philosophy of recording a song until it's perfect. We were all sayin' to each other, 'Okay, enough already. The song's good enough.' But at Motown, it wasn't a done deal until it was a perfect record."[27]

Berry Gordy not only took over management of the group, but he also took control of almost every aspect of their lives, including living arrangements. Joe, who had managed everything before, was left with little more to do than get the boys to rehearsal on time.

Gordy even relocated the family from Gary to the West Coast. In August 1969, Joe and the boys moved so they could record at Motown's new facilities in Hollywood while they went to school. Katherine and the rest of the children would join them in December, after Joe and the boys were settled into a house in Los Angeles that Gordy had leased for them. Initially, the West Coast Jacksons lived in motels: the Tropicana, a seedy place on Santa Monica Boulevard in Hollywood, then the Hollywood Motel, across the street from Hollywood High and closer to Motown headquarters. The accommodations were shoddy and inappropriate for young boys, but the Jacksons did not really care. After all, they were in sunny California, home to palm trees, orange groves, and movie stars; and anyway, since school had not yet started, they spent most of their time at the Motown studios rehearsing and recording test records.

Diana Ross

In October 1969 Gordy sent Michael to live with Diana Ross while he continued to move Joe and the boys from hotel to hotel. Gordy explained the move as calculated. Already, he had recognized Michael's extraordinary talent and had taken a special interest in him, grooming him for stardom: "People

After staying with her for a period of time, Michael Jackson became even more fascinated with Diana Ross.

think it was an accident that he stayed there. It wasn't. I wanted Diane [as Gordy called her] to teach him whatever she could . . . I knew Michael would pick up *something* just by being around her when she was home."[28]

Rather than just picking things up from Ross, Michael actively studied her. He later recalled:

> I remember I used to just sit in the corner and watch the way she moved. She was art in motion. Have you ever seen the way she works her hands? I was . . . *enthralled* with her. . . . I watched her rehearse one day in the mirror. She didn't know I was watching. I studied her, the way she moved, the way she sang, just the way she was. Afterwards, I told her, "I want to be just like you, Diane."[29]

Jackson was fascinated—some would say obsessed—with Diana Ross for years, and she has been an important influence in his life. (In fact, over the years rumors have persisted that Jackson first had plastic surgery because he wanted to look like Ross. He denies it.) From the start, Ross recognized and encouraged his talent. When she first met the Jacksons at Gordy's party, she told them that she would do whatever she could to assist them. And while Michael lived with her, she continually told him that he was going to be a great, great star. Jackson summed up his feelings, and her impact, in this way: "I'm crazy about her. She was my mother, my lover, and my sister all combined in one amazing person."[30]

Despite Michael's excitement about recording in California and living with Diana Ross, he missed his mother terribly. He had always been very close to Katherine and absolutely adored her. "The separation was most painful for Michael," Katherine remembered. "He was so sensitive as a boy."[31]

For her part, Katherine was afraid that her son, who had always shared her religious faith, would be corrupted in the house of this superstar with a reputation for egotism. Katherine had taught Michael that his talent was God's work and worried that he might lose sight of that and the values she had instilled in him. She need not have worried, though; she had done a good job and his values were stronger than the temptations.

Making It

Michael and his brothers essentially went from being completely under Joe's control to being completely under Gordy's. Gordy asked Suzanne de Passe, who had been with the Jacksons from the start as his assistant and was now president of Motown Productions, to help repackage the group—with new hairstyles, costumes, and so forth. Then they were ready for their first appearance on national television. On October 18, 1969, the Jackson Five appeared on the variety show *Hollywood Palace*, in an episode hosted by Diana Ross. The performance was a victory for the boys—particularly Michael, who astounded everyone. He had remarkable presence and control on stage, especially for someone so young. He reminded many of the multitalented Sammy Davis Jr. as a boy— a rare and complimentary comparison.

The Jackson Five were a sensation in everything they did. Their first singles, with Michael singing lead, were big hits. "I Want You Back" (October 1969) sold 2 million copies in six weeks and went to number one, as did "ABC" (March 1970), which sold 2 million in three weeks. The Jackson Five's first album, *Diana Ross Presents the Jackson Five*, sold 2 million copies almost immediately. Their third and fourth singles, "The Love You Save" (June 1970) and "I'll Be There" (Fall 1970), which sold over 2 million copies in three days and eventually sold a total of more than 3 million, also went to number one. This was the first time that a group's first four singles all became number-one hits.

The Jacksons benefited from arriving on the scene just when black pride was surging among the nation's young African Americans. But thanks to Gordy's genius and packaging, the group also appealed to the white market. In fact, on September 20, 1971, the Jackson Five received commendations from their congressman, entered in the *Congressional Record*, for their contributions to American youth. Michael and the Jackson Five had finally made it big, as evidenced by their appearance on *The Ed Sullivan Show*, the standard-bearer of popular culture at that time.

And the Jacksons were made for television. They went on
to appear on the most popular and most sought-after shows of
the day, including the *Tonight Show, American Bandstand, Soul
Train,* and *Hollywood Palace,* and were a hit every time. They
had exceeded even Gordy's dramatic predictions. Their concerts broke attendance records, with Michael stealing the
show. From the beginning it was clear that he would be the
star.

Chapter 3

The Down Side of Fame

FAME AND FORTUNE often go hand in hand. But fame can have a down side, as Michael soon learned. The more famous and popular the Jackson Five became, the more problems they had with increasingly uncontrollable fans and with trying to maintain their privacy and some semblance of a normal life.

Mob Scenes

Michael reacted much more dramatically to these problems than his brothers did. At the Jackson Five's first concert appearance for Motown on Saturday, May 2, 1970, at the Philadelphia Convention Center, it took one hundred police officers to keep the fans off the stage and three motorcycle-escorted limousines to get the group back to its hotel. The previous night there had been more than thirty-five hundred fans at the Philadelphia Airport to greet—and mob—the Jackson Five. When Michael finally got back to his room after the concert, he began to cry. Jermaine later explained: "Michael was scared to death. . . . The rest of us were more amazed than scared, but Mike was genuinely frightened."[32]

In July the Jackson Five performed at the Los Angeles Forum and broke attendance records. Deke Richards, the band's producer, was there with Berry Gordy and Diana Ross and recalled how the increasingly enthusiastic and uncontrollable fans were becoming a hazard:

> We almost got trampled to death. Before they started "The Love You Save," Michael said something like, "Here it is, the tune that knocked The Beatles out of

number one," and that caused sheer pandemonium. We were in the third row, and in the middle of the concert we heard this tumultuous sound and the rows were folding one at a time, people falling all over themselves. Someone ran onto the stage and got the kids off. They didn't even finish the song. Berry, Diana and I got out of our row just in time before it was toppled over by kids trying to get to the stage.[33]

As the Jackson Five's popularity increased, Michael came to fear and dislike the mobs of frenzied fans that followed the group.

A Natural

It was no mystery why the members of the Jackson Five were so popular and had such devoted fans. Extremely talented and appealing, particularly Michael, they seemed to cast a spell wherever they performed. In *Michael Jackson: The Magic and the Madness*, Lionel Richie, who toured with them in 1971, told biographer J. Randy Taraborrelli: "The only thing I can say I remember about that tour was the screaming crowds, and how amazing Michael was as a performer. For someone as young as he was, he had an amazing ability to entertain and make it seem so effortless."

Despite precautions such as twelve- and fourteen-foot-high stages, the Jackson Five were still rushed by overzealous fans. Even when they were not performing, wherever they went, the fans would somehow find and mob them. While on tour, the shopping excursions they loved became mob scenes that terrified Michael, as he later recounted:

Being mobbed by near hysterical girls was one of the most terrifying experiences for me in those days. I mean it was *rough*. We'd decide to run into some department store to see what they had, and the fans would find out we were there and would demolish the place, just tear it up. Counters would get knocked over, glass would break, the cash registers would be toppled. All we wanted to do was look at some clothes! When those mob scenes broke out, all craziness and adulation and notoriety became more than we could handle. . . . Those girls were *serious*. They still are. They don't realize they might hurt you because they're acting out of love. They mean well, but I can testify that it *hurts* to be mobbed. You feel as if you're going to suffocate or be dismembered. There are a thousand hands grabbing at you.[34]

Michael's fear and dislike of mobs and frenzied fans continued to grow as the number of tours increased. The Jackson Five started touring in the fall of 1970, but after their song "Never Can Say Goodbye" became a huge hit in 1971, they played forty-five cities during the summer. In such places as airports and hotel lobbies, the Jacksons received bruises, scrapes, and scratches, and had clumps of hair pulled out and pieces of clothing torn off. And there were occasions when Michael had to hide in closets or run through crowds of screaming girls with his hands covering his eyes to protect them. He maintains he still has scars that he can attribute to specific incidents in particular cities. Once, while touring England in 1972, Michael was almost choked when unruly fans were pulling on both ends of his scarf at the same time. He had to insert his hand under the scarf and start screaming to keep from being strangled. On that same tour, fans barricaded the entrance to the hotel where the boys were staying and did twelve-thousand-dollars' worth of damage to their limousine.

As the fans' behavior became more outrageous and aggressive, Michael became more withdrawn. To avoid public elevators in the hotels where they were staying, Michael's security man, Bill Bray, would often arrange for him to take the freight elevator. Ultimately while on tour, Michael would stay in his room, alone, when his brothers were sight-seeing, shopping, or out having fun.

The Move to Encino

On May 5, 1971, the Jackson family moved to a large estate in Encino, a wealthy community in southern California. The house, which was guarded by an electronic gate and a closed-circuit television system, had five bathrooms and six bedrooms, and Michael shared a room with Randy. On the two-acre estate was an Olympic-size swimming pool, a badminton court, a basketball half-court, and an archery range. There were also servant quarters, a guest house, a playhouse, and numerous trees and plants. The Jacksons soon added a hundred-thousand-dollar recording studio and a twenty-five-thousand-dollar darkroom. The house was lavish, and it was isolating. More and more the boys, particularly Michael, lived in a private world, sheltered from their fans and the hysteria. Increasingly, Michael was withdrawing, even from his family. Jermaine later recalled how the move to Encino affected the closeness the family had always maintained:

> We were real close when we had the other homes— before Encino. In Gary, we had two bedrooms—one for our parents and one for all of us. You *had* to be close. You felt that closeness as a family. But in Encino, the place was so big we had to make plans to see each other. I think that Michael, in particular, was unhappy there. He felt, as I did, that we were all losing touch with each other."[35]

The boys would never again be as close as they had been in Gary, when they were working together in pursuit of the fame and stardom they had finally attained.

Michael's Education

After they moved to Encino, even Michael's schooling contributed to his feelings of isolation. Previously, Michael had enjoyed attending fifth and sixth grades at Gardner Street Elementary, a public grade school in Los Angeles. He remembers the two years he spent there as a high point in his life, despite his inconsistent attendance caused by his work schedule. By the time that Michael entered Emerson Junior High, however, the Jackson Five had become so popular that he was forced to leave after only two weeks. Students were following him everywhere, and crowds would stand in the halls, just looking into his classroom. Worse yet, the school received a death threat against Michael. As a result, Joe and Katherine pulled him out of public school and enrolled him in a private one, which Michael detested. He refused to do his homework, was bored in class, and drew pictures of animals and monsters instead of listening to the teacher.

Because California law requires all minors to have at least three hours of schooling per day while they are working, Michael and the younger boys were tutored by Rose Fine, an accredited children's welfare supervisor, when they

Michael Jackson, age 13, displays some of the fan mail he received at the family's home in Encino, California.

were touring and unable to attend school. She was, according to Michael, a "wonderful tutor, who taught us a great deal and made sure we did our lessons. It was Rose who instilled in me a love of books and literature that sustains me today."[36] Much of Michael's traveling time was spent studying, and when he toured overseas, he earned educational credit. (Michael was eventually awarded a high-school equivalency diploma.)

Michael's life bore little resemblance to other young people's. He had no time for socializing or just hanging out because he was kept very busy with concerts, rehearsals, recording, and studies. But even beyond that, his isolation was another part of Motown's control. As Jermaine remembers: "When The Jackson 5 started getting success [Motown] kept us out of the public's eye on purpose as a strategy, to make a mystique, so we were never allowed to visit friends or go to a ball game. And that's bad for kids."[37]

Michael was learning the costs of the enormous fame that he and his brothers had achieved at such an early age. He talked about that double-edged sword with Oprah Winfrey when she interviewed him: "It was wonderful, there is a lot of wonderment in being famous. I mean you travel the world, you meet people, you go places, it's great. But then there's the other side, which I'm not complaining about. There is lots of rehearsal and you have to put in a lot of your time, give of yourself a lot."[38]

And that left no time for play, which is a necessary and natural part of most children's lives. Michael went on to tell Winfrey: "I remember going to the record studio, there was a park across the street and I'd see all the children playing and I would cry because it would make me sad that I would have to work instead."[39]

One time, when preparing to leave for a tour, Michael was missing when everyone else in the family was ready to go. They searched for hours and finally found Michael hiding and crying. He did not want to go on the tour; he wanted to go outside and play.

Not only was Michael robbed of his childhood but, ironically, many of his fans wanted, even expected, him to remain a child forever. Michael touched on that when, during her interview with him, Winfrey asked if adolescence was particularly difficult after being a child star. The performer replied: "Very. Very, very difficult, yes. Because I think every child star suffers through this period because you're not the cute and charming child that you were. You start to grow, and they want to keep you little forever."[40]

Michael, like most people, underwent dramatic changes during adolescence, particularly in his appearance. He grew from the cute little lead singer everyone knew, loved, and expected to see, into a lanky teenager. And he developed a terrible case of acne. Because of his visibility to the public and his sensitivity, these changes greatly undermined his self-image. Other peoples' negative reactions tended to reinforce his negative perception of himself. In his autobiography, *Moonwalk*, Jackson describes this:

> My appearance began to really change when I was about fourteen. I grew quite a bit in height. People who didn't know me would come into a room expecting to be introduced to cute little Michael Jackson and they'd walk right past me. I would say, "I'm Michael," and they would look doubtful. Michael was a cute little kid; I was a gangly adolescent heading toward five feet ten inches. I was not the person they expected or even wanted to see. Adolescence is hard enough, but imagine having your own natural insecurities about the changes your body is undergoing heightened by the negative reaction of others.[41]

Perhaps worst of all, Joe teased Michael about his pimples and repeatedly told him that he was ugly, making Michael cry daily. Michael became extremely self-conscious and depressed and withdrew even more.

> I became subconsciously scarred by this experience with my skin. I got very shy and became embarrassed to meet people because my complexion was so bad. It really seemed that the more I looked in the mirror, the worse the pimples got. My appearance began to depress me. . . . The effect on me was so bad that it messed up my whole personality. I couldn't look at people when I talked to them. I'd look down, or away.[42]

As he grew older, Jackson became more self-conscious and depressed over his physical appearance.

These changes in Michael's behavior and self-esteem served to accelerate a process that was already under way: The two sides of Michael's personality, indeed of his existence, were becoming more distinct and contradictory. Onstage he

was the consummate performer, displaying artistry and profes-
sionalism far beyond his years. Offstage he was childlike, running and playing like a small boy, attempting, it would seem,
to capture the childhood he never had. Onstage Michael felt
confident, at home, happy, and carefree. Offstage he felt in-
complete, inadequate, sad, and lonely. For Michael, the person
he became onstage was his true self. In an interview with biographer J. Randy Taraborrelli, Jackson describes this transformation:

> "When I'm not onstage, I'm not the same. I'm different,"
> [Jackson] observed. "I think I'm some kinda stage ad-
> dict. When I can't get onto a stage for a long time, I have
> fits and get real crazy. I start crying, and I act all weird
> and all freaked out. No kiddin', I do. I start to dancin'
> 'round the house."
>
> He began to talk rapidly. "It's like a part of me is missin'
> and I gotta get it back, 'cause if I don't, I won't be com-
> plete. So I gotta dance and I gotta sing, you know? I
> have this craving. Onstage is the only place I'm com-
> fortable. I'm not comfortable around . . . ," he paused,
> searching for the right word, "*normal* people. But when I
> get out onstage, I really open up and I have no prob-
> lems. Whatever is happening in my life don't matter no
> more. I'm up there and cuttin' loose and I say to myself,
> 'This is it. This is home. This is exactly where I'm sup-
> posed to be, where God meant for me to be.' I am un-
> limited when I'm onstage. I'm number one. But when
> I'm off the stage," he shrugged his shoulders, "I'm not re-
> ally. . . ." Again, he paused, trying to find the right word.
> "Happy."[43]

And there was something else that made Michael unhappy—
the way he was being recorded at the time. The Corporation was
still responsible for the Jackson sound and determined how
Michael would sing every song. As he grew older and more accomplished and confident, Michael often disagreed with the

group's decisions about his music, but he always sang the songs exactly as they wanted. He was tired of that and wanted more creative freedom.

One time, in 1972, while recording "Lookin' Through the Windows," Michael became so frustrated with the mechanical Corporation sound that he called Gordy and complained that they would not let him sing the song the way he wanted. Gordy immediately went to the studio and instructed producer Hal Davis to give Michael more freedom, but his creativity—and his growth—were still restricted. And Michael was still frustrated and dissatisfied.

Chapter 4

Breaking Away from Motown

MICHAEL HAD ALWAYS been cooperative—at first enthusiastically, then reluctantly—and deferred to Gordy and the Corporation, but he was tired of having to sing all of his songs exactly the way they wanted. Even at fourteen, he knew what he wanted to give to a song, but at Motown he was rarely allowed to. Michael was beginning to resent the Motown "method" and the almost total control that Berry Gordy had over him and the Jackson Five because it put a chokehold on his creativity and, in actuality, his career. Though the artist development division initially had helped make stars out of the Jacksons, as it had many Motown artists, the control that Gordy exerted kept them under his thumb. And Motown would not relinquish that control. In his autobiography, Jackson remembers: "They were continuing to mold us, keeping us from being a real group with its own internal direction and ideas. We were growing up and we were expanding creatively. We had so many ideas we wanted to try out, but they were convinced that we shouldn't fool with a successful formula."[44]

Motown's Formula Was No Longer Working

Assembly-line production was that formula, and it was growing less and less successful. Starting in April 1972 with "Little Bitty Pretty One," sales for the Jackson Five had been slipping, with each release selling fewer than the one before. Though the group was still popular, it was beginning to lose its audience.

The Corporation had split up over a disagreement, and as Deke Richards later said, "That was the beginning of the end of

The Jackson Five at Motown. After five years with the company, there was no direction any more."[45] But that was merely a problem with the quality in the production line. More important was Michael's desire for more creative control and the freedom to write his own songs. He knew that he had the talent and the ability, and he felt that he had earned the right.

Michael Jackson performs on stage. As time went on, Michael wanted more control over the quality of the songs he performed.

Joe Jackson, too, was upset with the falling sales and failing formula. The Jackson Five had not had a hit in quite some time. Joe, still believing strongly in his sons, blamed Motown and Gordy and was convinced that the records' poor sales were due to Motown's failure to promote and advertise them. When "Get It Together" was a hit in late 1973, it served to encourage Joe's confidence in the boys and in his belief that they would be more successful with a recording company that appreciated their talent and would work harder for them. "Dancing Machine," a single released in 1974, just after they returned from a successful tour of Africa, reinforced his position. It reached number two on the *Billboard* charts and sold over 2 million copies, the most singles sales for the group since "Never Can Say Good-Bye." More than ever, Joe felt that Motown was holding back Michael and the Jackson Five. He was not happy with the company's treatment of his boys and he, too, wanted them to be able to produce and have creative control of their records.

Family Problems Complicate Professional Problems

The family was experiencing personal problems as well as professional ones, which were contributing to Michael's unhappiness and confusion and were making it difficult for him to concentrate. Jermaine had married Hazel Gordy, Berry Gordy's daughter, at the end of 1973, and Jermaine was increasingly pulling away from his family. This was particularly troublesome for Michael because Jermaine was the brother he was closest to and was his best friend. While on tour, Michael roomed with Jermaine, and they shared many of the same interests. Likewise, onstage they stood next to one another, drawing on one another's support and energy. The two of them, of all the siblings, were most unlike Joe, which created an additional bond. Jermaine's withdrawal caused Michael to feel hurt, abandoned, and even more alone. Compounding this, Katherine and Joe were having serious marital difficulties, which profoundly disturbed Michael.

In March 1973, fed up with Joe's infidelity, Katherine had filed for divorce. This had really upset Motown because it con-

Marriage and the Jacksons

Marriage seemed to pose a problem for the Jacksons. Jermaine's marriage to Hazel Gordy had devastated Michael because it pulled his closest friend away from him. Later, when Jermaine sided with his father-in-law Berry Gordy Jr., it ripped apart the Jackson family. Earlier, in 1972, Tito had married Dee Dee Martes, despite his father's objections. Eventually, all of Michael's siblings would marry against their father's wishes, most of them young, as a way to defy and escape him. The only marriage that Joe Jackson did not oppose, ironically, was Jermaine's to Hazel—and it indirectly broke up the Jackson Five when Jermaine stayed with Motown. Eventually also, all of Michael Jackson's brothers' marriages would end in divorce after major problems and philandering and/or abuse.

tradicted the loving family image that Gordy had so carefully cultivated. The Motown executives wanted it kept a secret and badgered Katherine to reconcile for the sake of the family's image. Michael was devastated, and he was extremely angry at his father. When Katherine was planning to leave Encino, Michael wanted to go with her. He adored his mother and could not imagine staying at the family compound without her. Finally, partly due to the pressure Motown applied, Katherine dropped the divorce. She did leave for a few days but was back in time for Jermaine's wedding. It would have destroyed the family image had she not been there.

The Jacksons Take Vegas

All the while, the tension and competition between Joe and Gordy had been increasing. Joe wanted the boys to be something more than teen idols, and toward that end, he booked them at the MGM Grand in Las Vegas in April 1974. Gordy was opposed to the idea and told Joe: "You're makin' the biggest mistake of their career. What, are you crazy? These boys shouldn't be doing Vegas yet." Joe's reaction was telling. "Butt out! . . . These are *my* kids. Vegas has a good tradition, and I want them to know about it. It's time for them to grow."[46] Of course, each man wanted to prove himself right and the other wrong.

The Jackson Five added siblings LaToya, age seventeen, Randy, twelve, and Janet, seven, to their act, which was backed by the MGM Grand orchestra and Motown's rhythm section and featured Michael singing, dancing, and doing impressions. It also included impressions of earlier groups like the Four Freshmen and the Andrews Sisters. All of the Jacksons worked very hard, knowing that their performance and reception in Las Vegas was extremely important to their future. When they received a standing ovation on opening night, Gordy sent some executives to the hotel and delivered a prepared statement to the press declaring support and sharing in the triumph. Joe was livid, and the family felt betrayed. But Joe felt he had won that battle.

Joe also wanted the boys to start acting and worked with Raymond St. Jacques to have them star in a movie based on St. Jacques's screenplay *Isoman Cross and Sons.* Gordy opposed the idea because he did not think the boys could act (based on the Las Vegas comedic sketches, he was right) and because the screenplay

The Jackson family's dissatisfaction with Motown increased after their successful performances in Las Vegas (pictured).

required them to portray slaves. The film was never made; Gordy won that one. So went the tug-of-war.

The Beginning of the End

The Las Vegas shows gave the Jacksons creative control over their act for the first time, which fed their dissatisfaction with the conditions at Motown. They felt they had proved themselves, and they were tired of Motown holding them back. The time seemed right for change: Marvin Gaye and Stevie Wonder, two very talented and successful Motown artists, had finally been allowed to produce their own records and to publish their own songs. The Jackson Five wanted to do the same. Michael Jackson remembers how expressing the desire to write and produce was really the beginning of the end: "Our problems with Motown began around 1974, when we told them in no uncertain terms that we wanted to write and produce our own songs. Basically, we didn't like the way our music sounded at the time."[47]

Motown refused, saying the Jacksons still needed songwriters and producers. To make matters worse, Michael had begun releasing solo albums in 1972, and when his fourth one, *Forever Michael*, was released in January 1975, it did not do well. It was mediocre—nothing like what Michael was capable of and yearning to do. Furthermore, the boys were told they were not even allowed to mention, publicly or at Motown, that they wanted to produce and write their own songs. This really upset and discouraged Michael.

That, for Joe, was the final straw. He not only wanted his boys to write and produce their own material, he wanted them to establish their own publishing company so they would get the entire songwriter's royalty as well as the artist's. Gordy, of course, refused, so Joe decided they must leave Motown.

Michael Meets with Berry Gordy

Michael was miserable, as were his brothers, but he did not want his father to make a major decision like leaving Motown without consulting him. Michael had never been close to his father, and he had, in fact, always been frightened of him. In his interview with Oprah Winfrey, Jackson tells her: "There's been times

when he'd come to see me, I'd get sick, I'd start to regurgitate."[48]
Because of Joe's temper, beatings, and need for control, the tension and estrangement had steadily grown over the years and
had been compounded by Joe's infidelity. Michael did not trust
his father. But he did trust Gordy and hoped things could be
worked out. So he called Gordy to request a private meeting.
Michael admired and respected Gordy, realizing it was because
of him the Jacksons were where they were. By the same token,
Gordy realized that without Michael the Jacksons would not be
what they were, so he agreed to the meeting. Jackson remembers how difficult that meeting was:

> I went over to see him, face to face, and it was one of
> the most difficult things I've ever done. If I had been the
> only one of us who was unhappy, I might have kept my
> mouth shut, but there had been so much talk at home
> about how unhappy we *all* were that I went in and
> talked to him and told him how we felt. I told him I was
> unhappy.
>
> Remember, I love Berry Gordy. I think he's a genius, a
> brilliant man who's one of the giants of the music business.
> I have nothing but respect for him, but that day I was a
> lion. I complained that we weren't allowed any freedom to
> write songs and produce. He told me that he still thought
> we needed outside producers to make hit records.[49]

Gordy listened, and though he would not give Michael what
he wanted, he did promise that he would not do anything to hurt
Michael or his family. The meeting was significant not for what it
accomplished—essentially nothing—but for what it established:
Michael's importance. He got the meeting—something none of
his brothers would have been able to do—and he kept Gordy's
attention. And he stood up to him. Michael came away with new-
found confidence in himself, his abilities, and his power.

The Jacksons Leave Motown for Epic

After the meeting, Michael wanted to give Gordy another
chance. But Joe called a family meeting—excluding Jermaine,

When the rest of the Jackson Five signed a new recording contract with Epic Records, Jermaine decided to remain with Motown.

whom Joe considered untrustworthy because he was married to Gordy's daughter, and Randy, who was only thirteen. Michael was outvoted; his brothers were adamant about leaving Motown. And because of his loyalty to his brothers, Michael felt he must go along with them.

Performing Without Jermaine

Michael Jackson explains in the book *Moonwalk* what it was like performing without Jermaine.

> I clearly remember the first show we did without him, because it was so painful for me. Since my earliest days on the stage—and even in our rehearsals in our Gary living room—Jermaine stood at my left with his bass. I depended on being next to Jermaine. And when I did that first show without him there, with no one next to me, I felt totally naked onstage for the first time in my life.

Joe had been searching for another record deal and was interested in the CBS Records Group, particularly its Epic subsidiary, because of its commitment to black music. Ron Alexenberg, president of Epic, was very interested in the Jackson Five and thought they had immense unachieved potential. A deal worth about five hundred times the one at Motown was quickly cut and included the boys' option to choose three songs on each album, with songs they wrote to be considered. Michael was delighted and acknowledged: "This is one incredible deal. My father has done an amazing job for us."[50]

Jermaine Remains with Motown

The four other Jacksons, without telling Jermaine, signed with Epic before their contract with Motown had expired. When Joe confronted Jermaine and ordered him to sign, Jermaine refused. Ultimately, Jermaine had to choose between CBS and his father, and Motown and his father-in-law. He chose his father-in-law, leaving the Jackson Five. Michael Jackson remembered how conflicted they all were at that time: "We were relieved that we had finally made our feelings clear and cut the ties that were binding us, but we were also really devastated when Jermaine decided to stay with Motown."[51]

Michael agonized over the situation because he was closer to Jermaine, personally and professionally, than he was to any of his other brothers. Adding insult to injury, Motown, not the Jacksons, owned the name the Jackson Five, and Gordy had copyrighted it. Michael was hurt and angry and no longer trusted Gordy because he believed that, despite Gordy's promise, he had hurt Michael's family. Now Michael had pulled away from the two men who had controlled his life—his father and his mentor—and he had been abandoned by his best friend and big brother. Michael's feelings of emptiness, loneliness, and isolation were intensified.

Chapter 5

The Consummate Performer

THE EVENTS SURROUNDING Michael's departure from Motown made him feel sadder and emptier, more alone and isolated than ever. But when he was onstage, an amazing transformation would take place. Whatever was troubling or upsetting him ceased to exist. All that mattered to him was pleasing the audience. The negative things that haunted him seemed to become positive energy to fuel his performance, his gift to the audience. When the audience members responded—and they always did—he was elated. And he wanted to give them more. He wanted the performance to never end.

"Why does the show have to end? Why can't it just go on forever?"[52] Michael asked Jackie backstage, after three standing ovations. It was just hours after Jermaine had informed the family that he was staying with Motown, and the boys had performed magnificently. Michael had the audience eating out of his hand, despite the pain of Jermaine's defection. The stage, the performance, the audience: that was his reality. Pleasing the audience: that was what he lived for, what energized him, and what freed him from his upsets and concerns.

The Jacksons Variety Show

On June 30, 1975, Joe called a press conference to announce the Jacksons' move to CBS, but there were still more than eight months remaining on their contract with Motown, so they would be unable to record for CBS until the contract expired. In the meantime, in the public eye, the Jacksons kept up a good front and continued as usual—minus Jermaine. The group appeared on Carol Burnett's CBS variety show, with Randy filling in as the fifth Jackson, and he and Marlon lip-synched Jermaine's lines.

Behind the scenes, there were lawsuits that dragged on for four years while the bitterness and rivalry between Joe and Gordy persisted. First, there were the legal arguments over the name the Jackson Five. Ultimately Gordy won because Joe Jackson had not read the contracts (or even the parental guarantee agreement, promising he would make certain his sons abided by the terms of the recording contract) when he signed them. This blunder cost him and the boys dearly. Among other things, he had signed away all rights to the name.

Gordy also filed a lawsuit against Joe Jackson, the Jackson Five, and CBS for $5 million in damages for the group's having signed with CBS before the Motown contract had expired. Joe countersued, alleging Motown owed royalties, unpaid advances, and expenses. But according to the terms of the contract, the Jackson Five were liable for the costs of all of the songs they had

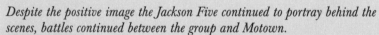

Despite the positive image the Jackson Five continued to portray behind the scenes, battles continued between the group and Motown.

recorded for Motown, even if they were never released. Michael and the Jackson Five had recorded an incredible 469 songs for Motown, but only 174 were released, so the group actually owed Motown over $500,000. Later Gordy amended the lawsuit, seeking an increased $20 million in damages after someone at CBS mistakenly used an old picture of the Jackson Five—with Jermaine—in an ad. After all was said and done, Gordy was awarded $600,000 in damages for advances that were not repaid, and compensation for Joe's not allowing the group to record for Motown when they were still under contract (a decision of Joe's that Michael had fought for ethical and business reasons), and for signing with CBS before the Motown contract had expired. The Jacksons left Motown with very little money and without their name.

In 1976 the Jacksons were offered their own television variety show, as a summer replacement. Michael was opposed to it from the beginning, believing it would damage their recording career, but he was outvoted once again. As he explains:

> It was a dumb move to agree to do that show and I hated every minute of it. . . .
>
> I think a TV series is the worst thing an artist who has a recording career can do. . . .
>
> It's a dead-end road. What happens is partly psychological. You are in people's homes every week and they begin to feel they know you too well. You're doing all this silly comedy to canned laughter and your music begins to recede into the background. When you try to get serious again and pick up your career where you left off, you can't because you're overexposed.[53]

The Jacksons had to wear what Michael referred to as ridiculous outfits and perform silly comedy skits, both of which embarrassed him. He knew he was not funny and did not think people should be put in a position where they were expected to laugh just because he was Michael Jackson. And he had to create three dance numbers a day. With tight schedules and deadlines,

Michael was not able to polish and perfect the numbers as he was accustomed to doing. After a four-week trial the show was renewed, but it was canceled due to poor ratings when it returned in January 1977.

Recording at Epic Records

Soon after that, in the spring of 1977, the group released its first album for CBS, *The Jacksons*, which included two songs that they had written and produced. They were not given free rein, as they had hoped, but at least it was a start. The Jacksons felt fortunate to have as their executive producers Kenny Gamble and Leon Huff, producers of the "Philly Sound," which had so successfully dominated the rhythm-and-blues and soul market in the 1970s, and Michael was learning all he could from them about production and songwriting, especially what he calls the "anatomy of a song."[54] The album, which was very positive and inspirational, was a big improvement over the final Jackson Five album and more effectively utilized the richness and more mature range and tone that Michael's voice was gaining with age.

By their third album, *Destiny* (December 1978), the Jacksons had written all but one of the songs. Michael sounded great, especially on the hit "Shake Your Body (Down to the Ground)," written by Michael and Randy, and the ballad "Push Me Away." His voice had matured, and he had become a brilliant stylist. *Destiny* was the Jacksons' first album to go platinum (ship one million copies). The Jacksons were once again on top. Los Angeles mayor Tom Bradley even declared "Jackson Day" in their honor.

Michael's Growing Business Sense and Influence

Meanwhile the family increasingly had been relying on Michael for business and creative decisions. In fact, it was because Joe had asked Michael to accompany him to a meeting with Ron Alexenberg at CBS headquarters that Peacock Productions had been formed. Skillfully, Michael had convinced Alexenberg that the Jacksons were ready to produce their own records, and as a result, *Destiny*, their best album to date, was Peacock's first effort.

Fantasyland

Even when Jackson was not performing, he still escaped from the
everyday world to a world of fantasy, dreams, and show business, as
he explains in this 1978 interview with biographer J. Randy
Taraborrelli, found in *Michael Jackson: The Magic and the Madness*:

> "How do you keep up with current events? Do you read news-
> papers? Watch TV?"

> "I watch cartoons," he told me. "I love cartoons." His eyes lit
> up. "I love Disney so much. The Magic Kingdom. Disneyland. It's
> such a magical place. Walt Disney was a dreamer, like me. And
> he made his dreams come true, like me. I hope."

> "What about current events?"

> Michael looked at me blankly. "Current events?"

> "Do you read the paper?" I repeated.

> He shook his head no. "See, I like show business. I listen to mu-
> sic all the time. I watch old movies. Fred Astaire movies. Gene
> Kelly, I love. And Sammy [Davis]. I can watch these guys all day,
> twenty-four hours a day. That's what I love the most. Show
> business, you know?"

Michael had developed a shrewd business sense. He was
astute and a quick study, absorbing and applying what he observed. And he had learned from the best. Earlier, when
Michael had learned of Gordy's having registered the name
the Jackson Five, he was in awe, even though the tactic had
been used against him. "I never even *thought* of that," he told
Jermaine. "I want to know how he did it. I'll have to remember all of this."[55] Also, Michael's one-on-one meeting
with Gordy had proven to him the value of negotiation and
communication. He was taking the first steps toward becoming the hard-headed, cunning businessman that would later
serve him so well.

Similarly, during those early years at Epic, Michael was de-
veloping a quiet authority, a presence, which everyone around
him noticed. James McField, the Jacksons' pianist and band director, observed how things were changing:

> He was still the soft, tender Michael Jackson everyone
> thought he was, but something was definitely differ-

ent. Everyone who dealt with him closely, family included, began to tread softly when dealing with Michael. The quiet power he was gaining was amazing to me. I'd never seen anyone have that much influence over people without having a stern attitude. I noticed that when he spoke, people were starting to listen.[56]

But in the family Michael was still often outvoted, even though he, for the most part, carried the group. Whether they did so out of jealousy, resentment, or shortsightedness, the brothers' uniting against Michael was fueling his estrangement from his family. He no longer had much in common with his brothers and felt they could not understand him or his ambitions. He did not want to answer to his father, and in fact, he did not even want to be around him. Michael wanted to make

Michael's feelings of detachment and resentment toward his family grew as his desire to be more independent increased.

Great Expectations

In *Michael Jackson: The Magic and the Madness*, Jackson admits to author J. Randy Taraborrelli that his personal and professional life are one, exposing once again how he "lives" onstage. He also reveals how alienated he was from his father, even though Joe maintained such control over his life, aspirations, and self-image.

We talked about old movies for a while, and about his involvement in *The Wiz*, the film he had just finished shooting in which he plays the Scarecrow. I asked what he saw as his biggest professional challenge.

"To live up to what Joseph expects of me."

"Joseph? Who's Joseph?" I wondered.

"My father. Joseph."

"You call your father by his first name?" I asked.

"Uh-huh."

"And living up to what he expects of you is a *professional* challenge?"

Michael mulled over my question. "Yes. A professional challenge."

"What about the personal challenges?"

"My professional challenges and personal challenges are the same thing," he said uneasily. "I just want to entertain."

his own decisions and do things on his own. He was branching out and taking on new challenges.

The Wiz

One of these challenges was acting in a film—something Michael Jackson had always wanted to do. He played the scarecrow in *The Wiz*, a remake of *The Wizard of Oz* set in contemporary Harlem, and he was totally captivated. This experience came at an opportune time, when Jackson was in the process of examining himself and exploring his options:

During this period in my life, I was searching, both consciously and unconsciously, I was feeling some stress and anxiety about what I wanted to do with my life now that I was an adult. I was analyzing my options and preparing to make decisions that could have a lot of repercussions. Being on the set of *The Wiz* was like being in a big school.[57]

Jackson was still having problems with his complexion, so he really liked wearing the required makeup. Even though the application took at least four hours to do, six days a week, Michael actually enjoyed the process. He explained why: "When I was transformed into the Scarecrow, it was the most wonderful thing in the world. I got to be somebody else and

Diana Ross starred as Dorothy with Michael Jackson (left) as the Scarecrow in the film The Wiz.

escape through my character."[58] Sometimes he even wore the makeup home at night.

Not only did he enjoy the change in his appearance, but Jackson also identified with the character he portrayed. In an interview with biographer J. Randy Taraborrelli, he explains his reasons for being drawn to the scarecrow:

> What I like about my character is his, I guess you could call it, his confusion. He knows that he has these, uh, problems, I guess you could call them. But he doesn't exactly know why he has them or how he got that way. And he understands that he sees things differently from the way everyone else does, but he can't put his finger on why. He's not like other people. No one understands him. So he goes through his whole life with this, uh, confusion.
>
> Everybody thinks he's very special. But really, he's very sad. He's so, so sad. Do you understand? Do you understand his sadness?[59]

While working on *The Wiz,* Jackson discovered a new talent, acting, and he also utilized a familiar one, dancing. On the set, Jackson learned the complicated dance routines with ease. Since early childhood, he had been able to watch a dance step, then immediately imitate it. But this ability created some problems because it embarrassed Diana Ross (who played Dorothy) and the other actors who could not learn the dance steps so easily. When Jackson realized this, he concealed his dexterity and tried to look like he did not always know what he was doing.

But even when things come easy to Jackson, he works hard. And he worked very hard on *The Wiz.* Because he is a perfectionist, Jackson demands a lot of himself, and as much as he loved what he was doing, it was still a stressful and anxious time for him. On July 4, while he was on the beach near Jermaine's house, a blood vessel burst in his lung. Jermaine had to rush him to the hospital. As Jackson explains: "It was suggested by my doctor that I try to take things a little slower, but my schedule would not permit it. Hard work continued to be the name of the game."[60]

Still, *The Wiz* was a good experience that gave Jackson new inspiration and strength. He discovered his love for acting and knew that he wanted to do more. Based on his performance in *The Wiz,* Jackson was offered the part of a transvestite in the movie version of *A Chorus Line,* but he refused it. For some time, there had been ongoing rumors and speculation that he was gay, despite his repeated and emphatic denials. Jackson felt that accepting the part would only exacerbate the problem, particularly since the offer came at a time when rumors were circulating that he was involved with singer/actor/songwriter Clifton Davis (who wrote "Never Can Say Good-Bye") and that was going to have a sex-change operation so they could marry. This rumor followed Jackson for quite some time.

At home, Jackson was still tormented by his appearance. His skin problems persisted, and he was extremely self-conscious about his nose, which he thought was too big. These insecurities were not helped by his brothers, who continually taunted him with the nickname "Big Nose," ignoring the pain and embarrassment this caused him. He talked about having surgery on his nose, but his father strongly opposed it: "I told him I'd break his face if he ever had it fixed. You don't fix something that ain't broke. He's got a great nose. It looks like mine."[61] But after Jackson fell and broke his nose in 1979, he had the first of what would become several rhinoplasties.

Off the Wall

Big changes were on the horizon in Jackson's professional life as well. He was discouraged and frustrated. He felt he had stopped growing professionally, and he did not like the Jackson Five image that the Jacksons had brought with them from Motown. He wanted to break away from the family and move on. So soon after *The Wiz,* Jackson began work on his first solo album for Epic. Wanting a sound different from the Jacksons, he teamed up with Quincy Jones. Jones, the music director for *The Wiz,* had begun his career as a fifteen-year-old trumpet player with Lionel Hampton and had gone on to arrange, compose, and produce for jazz legends such as Dinah Washington, Duke Ellington, Big Maybelle,

Tommy Dorsey, and Count Basie. He also had many successful pop and rhythm-and-blues albums and had composed scores for thirty-eight films. Jones and Jackson—both extremely talented and creative people who enjoyed mutual respect and admiration—worked wonderfully together. Jackson was delighted that Jones took his ideas seriously, and Jones recognized Jackson's brilliance. At a press conference Jones said: "Michael is the essence of what a performer and an artist are all about. He's got all you need emotionally, and he backs it up with discipline and pacing." And another time he predicted: "In my opinion, Michael Jackson is going to be *the* star of the eighties and nineties."[62]

Off the Wall, their first collaboration, became CBS Records' biggest-selling album and won one Grammy Award and three American Music Awards. Jackson became the first solo artist to have four top-ten hits from one album. People were paying attention. Jackson was on his way to becoming a superstar.

Chapter 6

Superstardom: The Agony and the Ecstasy

WITH THE INCREASED attention came increased public scrutiny and media coverage, particularly in the tabloids. At Motown, Gordy and his public-relations machine had been able to exert a tremendous amount of control over what was said about Jackson in the press. But at CBS there was no such control, and Jackson grew to mistrust the media. He hated being misunderstood, so even as he became more and more popular, he became more reclusive, giving fewer and fewer interviews. As Jackson later explained: "My biggest fear is being misquoted. One word can be cut into a statement and change the complete meaning and coloring of what was meant. Lately, people have been twisting everything I've been saying and that's why I shy away from many interviews."[63]

Jackson had no more control within his family than he had over the media. Though he essentially carried the Jacksons, he felt that his opinion did not matter and that he would always be outvoted. Even so, Jackson was still too tied to his family to completely pull away from them. Jackson felt lonely and alone. Both at home and at work, his life seemed totally out of his control.

The Struggle for Personal Control

Because Jackson could not change any of those things, at least not immediately, he focused on something that he could alter: his appearance. He had the second of his surgeries on his nose—ostensibly to correct breathing problems that resulted from the botched first surgery. The new narrower nose made Jackson feel a little better when he looked in the mirror, but not enough, and

Despite altering his physical appearance, Jackson was still obsessed with how he looked. Additionally, his feelings of loneliness and depression continued.

he already was talking about a third operation. Jackson became a vegetarian, which helped him clear up his skin and lose a lot of weight, giving him the dancer's body he wanted and making his face thinner and his cheekbones and jawline more prominent. Although his looks were altered dramatically, this was a temporary fix and served only to make him increasingly obsessed with his appearance. Jackson did not feel any better; he was still depressed and lonely: "Even at home, I'm lonely. I sit in my room sometimes and cry. It's so hard to make friends, and there are some things you can't talk to your parents or family about. I sometimes walk around the neighborhood at night, just hoping to find someone to talk to. But I just end up coming home."[64]

Turning to Others for Support

Over time, as Jackson pulled away from his family, he spent more time with and became closer to other celebrities. He had known actress Jane Fonda for a couple of years; impressed and delighted by his refreshing uncynical attitude, she was very protective of him. Sarah Holiday, Fonda's publicist for

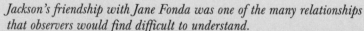
Jackson's friendship with Jane Fonda was one of the many relationships that observers would find difficult to understand.

the movie *On Golden Pond,* talked about Fonda's relationship
with Jackson:

> A lot of people thought that [their friendship] was very
> strange. But Jane just thought Michael was a fascinating
> person. She made it clear that if anyone were to ever gos-
> sip about her and Michael, that person would be in serious
> trouble. "He's too delicate to handle gossip," she would say.
> She had been in the business for so long, she said it was
> nice to talk to someone who seemed so unjaded by it all.[65]

That was just one of many relationships throughout Jackson's
life that were considered strange, even incomprehensible, by on-
lookers. He also became close to Fonda's father, actor Henry
Fonda, as well as to actors Katharine Hepburn and Marlon Brando.
And Jackson's close friendship with actress Elizabeth Taylor became quite well-known. Despite the age difference, these friend-
ships were the natural outgrowth of a common bond: These stars
had been in show business for years, so they shared many of the
same experiences, feelings, and attitudes. They understood media
hype, and they knew about overzealous fans; they had been the ob-
jects of public scrutiny, and they understood how the public per-

Ever the Perfectionist

Jackson's perfectionism is legendary. Even his spectacular performance
of "Billie Jean" on the NBC television special "Motown Twenty-Five:
Yesterday, Today, and Forever"—a performance most entertainers would
be thrilled with, a performance that has been called one of the twentieth century's greatest entertainment moments—was a disappointment.
Jackson remembers the performance in his autobiography, *Moonwalk.*

> I just remember opening my eyes at the end of the thing and
> seeing this sea of people standing up, applauding. And I felt so
> many conflicting emotions. I knew I had done my best and felt
> good, so good. But at the same time I felt disappointed in my-
> self. I had planned to do one really long spin and to stop on my
> toes, suspended for a moment, but I didn't stay on my toes as
> long as I wanted. I did the spin and I landed on one toe. I
> wanted to just stay there, just *freeze* there, but it didn't work
> quite as I'd planned.

sona can become confused with the private person. This is particularly true of Taylor because she had also been a child star and so understood the kinds of problems that Jackson faced. And these friends seemed to serve as a kind of surrogate family for Jackson when he needed them.

Another person whom Jackson turned to, not just for friendship but also to help extricate himself from his family, was John Branca, the entertainment attorney he had hired soon after he turned twenty-one and began taking charge of his professional life. Jackson wanted independence from Joe and the family, a contract as a solo artist, and more creative freedom. Jackson told Branca that he wanted to be the biggest star in show business and also the wealthiest. For more than ten years, Branca worked toward those goals. He negotiated all business deals and was a trusted friend and adviser who was crucial to advancing Jackson's career.

Becoming a Legend

Jackson's career not only took off, it skyrocketed. In December 1982 *Thriller* was released and went on to become the biggest-selling album in history. It broke one record after another in sales and popularity worldwide, as did two of its singles, "Billie Jean" and "Beat It," released in 1983. This was a dream come true—literally—for Jackson. In *Moonwalk,* he remembers:

> Ever since I was a little boy, I had dreamed of creating the biggest-selling record of all time. I remember going swimming as a child and making a wish before I jumped into the pool. Remember, I grew up knowing the industry, understanding goals, and being told what was and was not possible. I wanted to do something special. I'd stretch my arms out, as if I were sending my thoughts right up into space. I'd make my wish, then I'd dive into the water. I'd say to myself, "This is my dream. This is my wish," every time before I'd dive into the water.
>
> I believe in wishes and in a person's ability to make a wish come true. I really do.[66]

Jackson holds up the Grammy he won in 1984 for his record-breaking album Thriller.

When Jackson stole the show with his performance of "Billie Jean" on the NBC television special, "Motown Twenty-Five: Yesterday, Today, and Forever," sales of the album and the single shot through the roof. Jackson truly came into his own, with a new look, a new style, and an exhilarating performance. And that night, in front of an estimated 50 million people, Michael Jackson became a legend.

That legend, in his own time, made quite an impact. The moonwalk, a dance step that Jackson unveiled on the television special, became his signature step and a huge dance craze. His performance of "Billie Jean" sent a whole new segment of the population who had not been exposed to *Thriller* scurrying to buy the album. Once inside the music store, they often bought other albums as well. This was extremely important to an industry that was in the midst of a recession. Now Jackson not only had the all-time best-selling album, but he was also credited by many experts with reviving the sagging music industry. And later, because the "Billie Jean" single was so enormously popular, the "Billie Jean" video was finally played on MTV, and Michael Jackson was credited with breaking a color barrier and getting black artists on the MTV playlist. Jackson's "Motown Twenty-Five" performance was nominated for an Emmy, and "Motown Twenty-Five" won one. (At the end of the decade Jackson's performance would be included in *Entertainment Weekly* magazine's list as one of the twentieth century's greatest entertainment moments.) In *Billboard's* 1983 recap, Michael Jackson was named the top artist in categories of pop, black, and dance/disco music, and *Thriller* was number one and "Billie Jean" and "Beat It" were number one or two on many of the charts. And at the 1984 Grammy Awards, Jackson won a record number of awards, seven for *Thriller,* with an eighth for his narration of the children's album *E.T.*

Retreating

As Jackson became more celebrated and more in control of his professional life, his love-hate relationship with his fans intensified. "I love my fans," he told photojournalist Dave Nussbaum, "but I'm afraid of them. Some of them will do anything to get to you. They don't realize that what they are doing might hurt you."[67] Meanwhile, in late 1982, Jackson had demolished and started a two-year rebuilding of the house in Encino, of which he was now half owner, having bought his share when Joe was having financial difficulties. He created a self-contained world—an escape from the outside world and the pawing, grabbing, demanding fans he so feared.

The Tudor-style house included a three-room picture gallery with themes of early Jackson family memorabilia, Jackson Five history, and Jackson as an adult; stables for his collection of animals that roamed the backyard during the day; a pool, fountain, and Jacuzzi; and a thirty-two-seat theater with red velvet seats. The house also featured a replica of Disneyland's Main Street with puppet characters that Jackson described as being "like real people. Except they won't grab at you or ask you for favors." Jackson explained that he "put all this stuff in so I will never have to go out *there*."[68] He even had five life-size female mannequins posed in different parts of his bedroom. As he explained to biographer J. Randy Taraborrelli:

> I guess I want to bring them to life. I like to imagine talking to them. You know what I think it is? Yeah, I think I'll say it. I think I'm accompanying myself with friends I never had. I probably have two friends. And I just got them. Being an entertainer, you just can't tell who is your friend. So I surround myself with people I want to be my friends. And I can do that with mannequins. I'll talk to them."[69]

At the same time that he was retreating from the outside world, Jackson was also distancing himself from his family both emotionally and professionally. In 1983, after much soul searching and with much difficulty, he fired his father. After all of those years, Joe Jackson would no longer be representing his son. Joe was hurt and angry, and Michael's action widened the chasm between father and son. Partly, Jackson had fired his father because he did not agree with him or support his ideas. And, of course, Jackson wanted control over his own life and career. But it was also because Jackson was so upset and angry with his father over his infidelities and wanted to punish him. He did not even want to be around Joe and tried to avoid him. When he could not, there would usually be a loud argument and Jackson would end up running to his room.

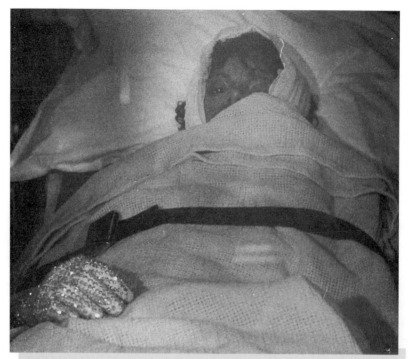

Michael Jackson arrives at the hospital after suffering second-degree burns while filming a Pepsi commercial.

The *Victory* Tour

Jackson's estrangement from his family was so severe that he initially refused to join his brothers on a Pepsi-sponsored tour, the *Victory* tour, scheduled for 1984. Whereas before feelings of loyalty would have interceded and he would have relented, this time he was adamant for a long time. But he could not hold out against his mother. Finally, against his better judgment, he gave in to her pleas and agreed to go. As part of the promotion, Jackson made some commercials for Pepsi.

In the second one, his hair caught fire during one of the special effects and he was rushed to the hospital—weakly waving to the media with his trademark one-gloved hand. The accident became the lead story on all of the evening news broadcasts, and it was covered extensively. The hospital where he was taken for treatment had to add six volunteers to answer the phone calls from well-wishers, and thousand of calls, letters, and cards poured in, including a letter from President Ronald Reagan. The extent of the publicity and the tremendous public response were evidence of how popular Michael Jackson had become.

There were many problems behind the scenes with the *Victory* tour, including problems with Don King, the promoter; with ticket sales; with management; and with the tour's overall organization. But there were none with the shows themselves, which were sensational. And more than ever, Jackson lived to be onstage. That was where he felt comfortable, confident, and complete, transformed into the person he was meant to be.

Between shows he spent time in his room making videos of himself, studying tapes of his performance, or practicing on a portable dance floor that he carried with him—just waiting for his next performance, when he would come alive again. During breaks in the tour, he went to Disneyland, his favorite place, whenever he could. He spent little, if any, time with his brothers. And even onstage, a distance—awkwardness, even—was evident among them. They had little in common any more. Jackson had agreed to the tour for the sake of the family, and it had only driven him further away.

Failed Intimate Relationships

Family problems, such as Jackie's extramarital affair with former Laker cheerleader, choreographer, and dancer Paula Abdul and sister Janet's ill-advised marriage to singer James DeBarge, did not help the estrangement. Jackson was already tormented by his father's repeated unfaithfulness to his mother and how deeply it had hurt her and had damaged their marriage. And his brothers' marriages, with all of their infidelities, disturbed him deeply. As a result, Jackson became even more skeptical and frightened of intimate relationships. For many years, he swore he would never marry because of all of the infidelity, pain, and hypocrisy that he had witnessed: "I don't understand my family. And I don't like some of the things my brothers do to their wives. I'm never going to marry. I just can't take it. It's awful, marriage. I don't trust anyone enough for that."[70]

For whatever reason, Michael seemed unable to have an intimate relationship. He offers an acknowledgment and one explanation in his autobiography, *Moonwalk:*

> My dating and relationships with girls have not had the happy ending I've been looking for. Something always seems to get in the way. The things I share with millions of people aren't the sort of things you share with one. Many girls want to know what makes me tick—why I live the way I live or do the things I do—trying to get inside my head. They want to rescue me from loneliness, but they do it in such a way that they give me the impression they want to share my loneliness, which I wouldn't wish on anybody, because I believe I'm one of the loneliest people in the world.[71]

Jackson did have a few widely reported relationships, but opinions vary on how serious they were. In *Moonwalk,* he describes actress Tatum O'Neal as his first real date and says, "I fell in love with her (and she with me) and we were very close for a long time."[72] But O'Neal has always maintained that they were just friends. Jackson also calls actress Brooke Shields "another love" and says: "We were romantically serious for a while."[73] She, too, denies anything more than friendship.

To the public, these relationships appeared to be publicity setups. In fact, in the biography *Michael Jackson: The Magic and the Madness,* Taraborrelli relates the background of two of Jackson and Shields's most notable dates. On February 7, 1984, Jackson was inducted into the *Guinness Book of World Records* because *Thriller* had broken all records for album sales. CBS Records held a black-tie party in his honor, and, as Taraborrelli tells it: "Michael was accompanied by actress Brooke Shields. *Her* 'people' had gotten in touch with *his* 'people' and suggested that she would be the perfect date. 'Why not?' Michael decided."[74]

Shields also accompanied Jackson to the Grammy Awards on February 24. According to Taraborrelli, Shields stopped by the house to ask if Jackson would take her. He did not want to, but he allowed her to talk him into it. Later, he told an employee, "She's

okay, . . . but I only took her to help her out, . . . there was no ro-
mance. Not at all. We're friends. All of this was strictly for her, for
the sake of publicity. She's nice. I like to help her out when I can.
It was good P.R. for her to be seen with me."[75] Jackson's sexuality
had been the subject of media speculation and rumors for years,
and it appeared to many that his Grammy appearance with
Shields was intended to help squelch the rumors.

Jackson adamantly denied that he was gay, but it did not seem
to help. After a tabloid reported that he was having an affair with
British pop star Boy George, Jackson decided to respond. He
arranged a major news conference with a prepared statement, read
by his manager, Frank Dileo, addressing some of the rumors that
were circulating. Jackson denied taking hormones to maintain his
high voice, denied having had his cheekbones altered, denied having had cosmetic surgery on his eyes, and declared his plans to get
married and have a family in the future. He also threatened to in-
stitute legal action and prosecute to the fullest extent of the law for
any "new fantasies" that were printed.

Although Jackson declared his heterosexuality in the statement, he did not deny or confront the rumors and repeated reports of his alleged homosexuality. And since Jackson did not
even attend the news conference and was not forthcoming about
his surgeries in the prepared statement, the news conference did
not accomplish what he had intended and actually raised more
questions than it answered.

Other Projects

But as always, Jackson kept working. After the *Victory* tour, he
was able to work on a project that combined two of his special
interests—his hero, Walt Disney, and the movies—when the
Disney Studios asked him to do a film. *Captain Eo*, produced by
Francis Ford Coppola and directed by George Lucas, is, according to Jackson: "about transformation and the way music can
change the world."[76] Using spectacular special effects, the movie,
is a celebration of good over evil. In *Moonwalk*, Jackson goes on
to explain: "Working on *Captain Eo* reinforced all the positive
feelings I've had about working in film and made me realize
more than ever that movies are where my future probably lies."[77]

Despite the problems in his personal life, Jackson continued his work on numerous music projects.

Then, in early 1985, Jackson—along with forty-five of the biggest musical stars—recorded "We Are the World," a song Jackson had written with singer/songwriter Lionel Ritchie to raise money for relief to Africa. All proceeds were to go to the nonprofit group USA for Africa to provide emergency food, medical relief, and self-help programs to Ethiopia and other areas of Africa that were devastated by a terrible famine.

The project was important to Jackson, and despite his shyness and discomfort around others, he was instrumental in uniting the diverse assemblage of stars and inspiring them to play a part in fighting world hunger. The artists were energized by the project and excited about working with one another; they felt uplifted and shared a strong sense of community. But Jackson was not a part of it. He stayed separate and aloof, never taking off his sunglasses. It was as though he were erecting an invisible barrier between himself and the others. His solo was even taped later, privately, and spliced in. Jackson's isolation and eccentricities were becoming more and more consuming.

Chapter 7

The Public Image: Eccentricities and Ridicule

IN THE YEARS following the phenomenal success of *Thriller*, Michael Jackson's reputation as an eccentric grew. Controversy surrounded him at nearly every turn, in both his professional and private lives, much of it brought on by his own miscalculations.

Yet behind the weird public image exists a generous humanitarian who still adheres to the strict religious principles with which he was raised, contradicting the image of the stereotypical hard-drinking, hard-living rock star. And there are little-known facets of Jackson that reveal the complex person he is. Unlike many other rock stars, Jackson is the enormous success and beloved star that he is despite his public image, rather than because of it.

Bad

One source of controversy was Jackson's album *Bad*, which was finally released in August 1987, after two and a half years of work and many delays. The delays were caused by Jackson's legendary perfectionism as well as the pressure of making the follow-up to the biggest-selling, most-celebrated album of all time. *Bad* debuted at number one on the *Billboard* charts, making Michael Jackson only the fifth artist ever to debut at number one. And even though it was released fairly late in the year, *Bad* was still the top-selling album of 1987.

But *Bad* proved controversial despite its commercial success. Jackson had a new look: he wore all black, his clothes were adorned with buckles, buckles, and more buckles; his hair was longer, and he sported a newly chiseled cleft in his chin. During performances on the *Bad* tour, and in the video for the title track, Jackson apparently attempted to look and act "bad," stamping his feet, shouting, shaking, and repeatedly grabbing his crotch. Some critics speculated that these actions were meant to establish Jackson's masculinity and counter the persistent rumors about his sexuality. Instead, Jackson was ridiculed and satirized. And many in the black music community felt that the title track conveyed stereotypes that were offensive to African Americans.

Hurt by all of the bad press that he was receiving, Jackson wrote an open letter to *People* magazine that was published while he was on tour:

> Like the old Indian proverb says, do not judge a man until you've walked 2 moons in his moccasins [sic]. Most people don't know me, that is why they write such things in wich [sic] most is not true. I cry very very often because it hurts and I worry about the children. All my children all over the world, I live for them. If a man could say nothing against a character but what he can prove, his story could not be written. Animals strike not from malice, but because they want to live, it is same with those who criticize, they desire our blood, not our pain. But still I must achieve. I must seek truth in all things. I must endure for the power I was sent forth, for the world, for the children. But have mercy for I've been bleeding for a long time now. MJ[78]

And things continued to deteriorate for Jackson. In *Rolling Stone* magazine's yearly poll, he was voted the worst artist in almost all categories. Even with four nominations, Jackson did not win a Grammy Award that year, in contrast to 1984, when he had received a record eight. He was terribly hurt and depressed.

Jackson's stage antics during the Bad *tour and his numerous plastic surgeries became the subject of widespread criticism and ridicule.*

Sources of Ridicule

Jackson was also upset about the public's ongoing preoccupation with his appearance. It was obvious that his face had been altered surgically, but Jackson has admitted to only three surgeries: two on his nose and one to add the cleft in his chin. Not only has he denied any additional work, but he has also resented the implication:

All of Hollywood has plastic surgery! I don't know
why they point me out. The press exaggerated it. It's
just my nose, you know. They want it to be everything.
Just the nose isn't enough. Elvis had his nose done—
Lisa Marie (Presley's daughter and Jackson's ex-wife)
told me. They don't talk about that. They single me
out. It's not fair.[79]

Many theories were proposed to explain why Jackson had
altered his appearance so drastically. Some observers suggested
that Jackson seemed to be trying to appear more "white"; meanwhile, others believed he was trying to achieve the perfect face
or resemble his idol, Diana Ross. Still others speculated that he
was trying to erase any resemblance to his father. Whatever his
motivation or intent, Jackson's numerous surgeries have evoked
widespread public scrutiny and derision.

So have the bizarre stories about him that have been repeatedly circulated. Few people realize, however, that Jackson
himself initially was responsible for promoting and planting
many of those stories to garner publicity. At one point, in an
attempt to further his career, Jackson gave his attorney, John
Branca, and his manager, Frank Dileo, a book about the philosophy of P. T. Barnum, a showman known for saying,
"There's a sucker born every minute." Barnum thought that
most people were gullible and would believe almost anything,
and he used this theory to exploit situations and to convince
people that the circus he ran was, as advertised, "the greatest
show on earth." Jackson told Branca and Dileo, "This is going
to be my Bible and I want it to be yours. I want my whole career to be the greatest show on earth."[80] Soon, Jackson began
putting Barnum's theory to the test.

While filming *Captain Eo*, Jackson had faked an injury to generate publicity. When the strategy worked, he took it a step further:
with assistance, he planted the now-notorious hyperbaric-chamber
story and picture. When Jackson was hospitalized for the burns
he had suffered while filming the Pepsi commercial, he had seen
a hyperbaric chamber, a casket-size machine used to help heal
burn victims. With an atmosphere of 100 percent oxygen under

increased pressure, the chamber is designed to flood body tissues with oxygen. Jackson became fascinated with it, wondering if it might prolong life. At first he wanted to buy one, but Dileo talked him out of it, so he decided to have his picture taken in it. It was then Jackson's idea to plant the story that he wanted to sleep in the chamber so he could live to be 150 years old, and that he would be taking it with him on the next tour. He did not know if anyone would believe the story, but he wanted to find out. So Dileo contacted a reporter for the tabloid *National Enquirer*, told him the story, and provided a picture of Jackson in the chamber. The story was printed—repeatedly—and believed. Jackson was astonished. "I can't believe that people bought it. It's like I can tell the press anything about me and they'll buy it. We can actually control the press. I think this is an important breakthrough for us."[81]

Next came the story of the pursuit of the remains of John Merrick. Merrick, a nineteenth-century Englishman, was known as "the Elephant Man" because he suffered from a rare disorder that hideously deformed his face and body. His story, told in the movie *The Elephant Man*, moved Jackson to tears with its depiction of Merrick as an outsider searching for love and acceptance. Jackson became interested in Merrick's medical condition when he began reading medical books after he was burned. To see what kind of publicity he could get, Jackson decided to offer to buy Merrick's remains from the hospital where they were kept. As with the hyperbaric-chamber story, the stunt received a tremendous amount of publicity, and Jackson was delighted. Here was a way to get back at, to control, the press he so despised.

Michael Jackson on Being Michael Jackson

In *Moonwalk*, Jackson explains what motivates him:

> To me, nothing is more important than making people happy, giving them a release from their problems and worries, helping to lighten their load. I want them to walk away from a performance I've done saying, "That was great. I want to go back again. I had a great time." To me, that's what it's all about. That's wonderful.

Though the planted stories did, as Jackson intended, generate publicity for him and temporarily give him a sense of power over the press, they did not pique people's interest or entice them to learn more, as he had hoped. Instead, they only convinced people that Jackson was so weird that he had lost touch with reality. This hurt him deeply. The strategy was a gross miscalculation, and in the long run it hurt his image and his career.

Jackson's strategy backfired further when unprincipled journalists started creating stories about him in addition to those he planted himself. The sensational stories always sold a lot of magazines and newspapers, and once Jackson had painted himself with the "weird" brush, people would believe just about anything. So, according to published reports, Jackson had built a shrine to Elizabeth Taylor, where her movies played twenty-four hours a day; he had asked her to marry him; he had tried to convince her to sleep in the hyperbaric chamber with him; he was certain the world was going to end in 1998; he refused to bathe in anything but Evian water; he was going to perform behind a Plexiglas shield while on tour to protect himself from germs; and he had seen the ghost of legendary musician John Lennon.

All of these stories were untrue, and all upset Jackson tremendously. What he did not seem to understand was that he was the one who had started the ball rolling. When an associate tried to explain to Jackson that he could not plant false stories and then become upset when the media could not differentiate between his false stories and others' rumors, Jackson responded, "It's different if I say it's true and it's not, but I don't like it when other people say things about me that are untrue. That's not fair."[82] And his refusal to grant interviews to clarify or deny the rumors kept the stories alive, as did his idiosyncratic behavior. The false or embellished stories often did not seem any stranger than those known or proven to be true, so they, too, were simply accepted as fact. Jackson's behavior convinced the public that he was very bizarre, particularly when his actions did not seem to conform to his explanations.

One of the most blatant examples is Jackson's well-publicized use of disguises. As he became more reclusive, he would rou-

Many of the stories and rumors about Michael Jackson were begun by the artist himself in an attempt to generate publicity.

tinely wear a disguise when he did venture out. In an interview for *TV Guide*, he explains: "I do disguises for different reasons. . . . I like to study people—be like the fly on the wall. Even if it's two old ladies sitting on a bench or some kids on a swing. Because I don't know what it's like to fit in an everyday situation."[83] Another reason he gave for the disguises was that they allowed him to go about his business without being recognized. That does not seem so strange. After all, he had no privacy, and he certainly was one of the most recognizable men in the world. But usually the disguises would be so outrageous that he would be certain to be recognized, and he would create even more of an uproar, getting more attention than if he had gone undisguised.

After Jackson had his fourth surgery on his nose in 1986, he would wear a surgical mask with a black fedora and sunglasses—or a gorilla mask—when he went out. This made him extremely conspicuous and reinforced his image as a kook. The media said—and it was generally believed—that he was wearing a mask to avoid catching germs, allegedly his latest obsession. Jackson did not comment publicly on these stories, but privately he said that he was wearing a mask because he had had his wisdom teeth pulled. In fact, he had just had the cleft put in his chin.

Another well-known and frequently discussed trait is Jackson's love of animals. In her interview, Oprah Winfrey asked Jackson why he was so fascinated with animals, and he responded: "Because I find in animals the same thing I find so wonderful in children. That purity, that honesty, where they don't judge you, they just want to be your friend. I think that is so sweet."[84] His menagerie has included deer, a llama, a horse, a sheep, swans, birds, snakes, tarantulas, giraffes, a lion, and his most famous pet, Bubbles the chimpanzee. Many people think it odd to have such a collection of animals, most of which are not traditional pets. But his attachment to Bubbles has been especially mocked and ridiculed. Bubbles reportedly had his own room in Jackson's house and a crib in Jackson's room. He also had an entire wardrobe that included designer clothes. Bubbles accompanied Jackson on his solo tour to Japan, where he had his own hotel room that Jackson had rewallpapered because Bubbles is sensitive to cigarette smoke. For a while, everywhere Jackson went, Bubbles went, too; it seemed they were inseparable. This confirmed Jackson as—at the very least—a screwball in the minds of most observers. And here, as was the case with his other eccentric behavior, what was observed in public invited speculation about what went on in private, eliciting further ridicule.

Perhaps the characteristic most discussed and ridiculed in the press was Jackson's childlike—some would say childish—behavior and his attempts to surround himself with the trappings of childhood. While on the *Bad* tour, he closed the deal on a ranch in the Santa Ynez Valley, which he soon renamed Neverland Valley. The ranch, also called Neverland, is an amusement park, a playland stocked with animals, toys, and things designed for children. It is a place where, despite being one of the richest and most powerful entertainers in the world, Jackson can act like a child. Some people believe this behavior is Jackson's way of experiencing the childhood he never had. Others have been baffled, and some disturbed, by Jackson's seeming to pretend to be a child and by his relationships with children.

Controversy and Scandal

Over the years, Jackson has had several public—and controversial—relationships with young boys. Child actor Emmanuel Lewis frequently traveled with Jackson until Lewis's mother, concerned when they registered at a hotel as father and son, stepped in. And Jackson took ten-year-old Jimmy Safechuck to London on the *Bad* tour. This relationship appeared suspicious to many, especially when Jackson gave the boy's parents a $100,000 Rolls Royce. There have been other relationships as well, but the controversy reached its peak in 1993, when Jackson was charged in a lawsuit with sexually molesting an adolescent boy. There were charges and countercharges, escalating accusations and adamant denials–all covered explicitly, extensively, and sensationally by the media. Finally, the case was settled out of court, with Jackson paying a settlement reputed to be between $10 and $20 million.

Law enforcement officials tried to pursue the case in spite of the settlement, but the boy refused to testify. In 1994, after a thirteen-month investigation in which 400 witnesses were interviewed, the formal investigation was concluded, no charges were filed, and the case was closed. The statute of limitations ran out in 1999, so it is unlikely that the truth of what happened will

Michael Jackson's public relationships with young boys have been the subject of much controversy and scandal.

ever become public knowledge. Some people believe strongly that Jackson is a pedophile and that this boy was just one of many. Others believe that the accusations were fabricated to extort money from Jackson, and they point to the inability of law enforcement officers to find any proof of Jackson's misconduct as confirming his innocence.

Marriage

Less than a year after settling the case, Jackson shocked the world by marrying Lisa Marie Presley, daughter of music legend Elvis Presley. Predictably, the marriage was greeted with skepticism. Some critics speculated that it was a publicity stunt. Others believed it was an attempt to prove that Jackson was, in every way, a normal adult male. Still others thought it was a way for Jackson to get his hands on the publishing rights to Elvis Presley's songs. Very few believed the marriage was genuine, and most predicted a quick divorce. Sure enough, despite their protestations of true love in a nationally televised interview with journalist Diane Sawyer, the two were divorced after only eighteen months.

In November 1996 came another shocker: Deborah Rowe, an assistant to Jackson's plastic surgeon, was pregnant with Jackson's child. The reaction was predictable—Rowe must have been artificially inseminated. The couple denied it and were married in Australia three months before the baby, Prince

Many critics correctly predicted that Jackson's marriage to Lisa Marie Presley would not last very long.

Michael Jackson Jr., was born. A little over two years later, a second child, Paris Michael Katherine, was born. But Jackson's second marriage, like his first, was doomed to failure. In October 1999, Jackson and Rowe filed for divorce.

Behind the Public Image

Jackson's two marriages did little to counter the negative public image established by his continuing relationships with young boys, the bizarre stories he had planted in the press, his abnormal behavior and appearance, and his *Bad* persona—obvious errors in judgment that have hurt him professionally.

Jackson's marriage to Deborah Rowe lasted only three years.

Among close friends and associates, however, Jackson is known as a shrewd and astute businessman. As John Branca, Jackson's former attorney, tells *Billboard:* "The genius in his artistry speaks for itself. His business acumen isn't necessarily as obvious because it is conducted behind closed doors. But he is equally brilliant in running his career as he is in recording his music."[85]

Walter Yetnikoff, president of CBS Records, has said that he believes that Jackson would be totally qualified to run a record company if he wished. In light of this praise, some of Jackson's decisions appear even stranger. And these miscalculations have cost him dearly. Ironically, Jackson's own reclusiveness and reluctance to grant interviews—both of which have grown over the years—prevent him from countering the "weird" label that is attached to him. But behind that label and beyond the image are attributes and deeds that reveal another, seldom-seen side of Jackson.

Faith and Good Works

One of the constants in Jackson's life that has largely gone unpublicized is his faith and adherence to religious principles. Jackson was raised as a Jehovah's Witness, even though his father, to his dismay, did not practice the religion. Jackson was a dedicated follower as a child and teen, and at sixteen, an age when many young people are questioning or rebelling, Jackson would lecture on God and religion at any opportunity, to anyone who would listen. Although all of the Jackson children attended Kingdom Hall (their place of worship) when young, Michael was the one who attended most frequently with his mother after they were grown. Each Jehovah's Witness is considered an ordained minister and is expected to attempt to convert others, so even at the peak of his popularity in the mid-1980s, Jackson would go door to door in disguise, proselytizing. Although he left the church in 1987 due to conflicts between its strict tenets and his lifestyle as an entertainer, he continued to follow its prohibitions against drugs and alcohol.

Another tenet of the Jehovah's Witness religion is an emphasis on good works. While Jackson is undoubtedly one of the wealthiest individuals in the world and enjoys a lavish lifestyle, he has also been exceptionally generous, about which he has remained virtually silent. He has set up and funds numerous foundations and contributes liberally to a number of charities. In fact, Jackson appears in the *Guinness Book of World Records* for the most charities supported by a pop artist, with a total of thirty-nine. He donated his share of the proceeds from the *Victory* tour (approximately $5 million) to three charities and the proceeds for the *Bad* tour ($600,000) to the United Negro College Fund. Additionally, he has opened Neverland to hundreds of seriously ill and dying children, furnishing an entire floor to provide for their special needs. And he sets aside tickets to his concerts for underprivileged children who would otherwise not be able to attend.

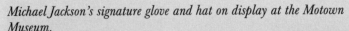

Michael Jackson's signature glove and hat on display at the Motown Museum.

Jackson in the Nineties

In his professional life, Jackson continued to record throughout the nineties, still generating controversy. The video for the single "Black or White," from the *Dangerous* album released in 1991, caused an uproar with its violent images of Jackson smashing car windows and repeatedly grabbing his crotch. He ended up cutting four minutes from the video to remove the offensive material. And the song "They Don't Care About Us," off the 1995 *HIStory* album, was perceived by many to be anti-Semitic, despite Jackson's insistence to the contrary. Controversies aside, however, Jackson has continued to achieve success with his music in the United States, and especially internationally, although he has never regained the formidable popularity he attained with *Thriller.*

Entertainer of the Decade: Accomplishments and Accolades

T HOUGH THE SUCCESS of *Thriller* would have been enough to include Jackson among the most influential entertainers of the 1980s, his contributions extend far beyond that. Time and again, Jackson was recognized and honored as the entertainer of the decade. President George Bush even honored him with an "Artist of the Decade" award in a White House ceremony. *Billboard*'s recap (December 23, 1989) accurately and artfully states the consensus:

> Michael Jackson was both the hottest and most immediately influential artist of the 80's. The Gloved One was far and away the top artist of 1983 in pop, black, and dance music, and also had the top album in all three formats, *Thriller*. . . .
>
> Jackson's success confirmed once and for all the sales potential of black music and opened the door for other black artists. And many follow his lead.[86]

And *People* magazine, in its retrospective of the 1980s, included Jackson as one of the twenty people who helped define the decade. But even beyond that, *Ebony* magazine includes

Jackson as one of the twenty-five who changed American music. This is why:

> Michael Jackson is hailed as the "King of Pop," but it is in the realm of music videos that his impact has been

President George Bush honors Michael Jackson for his musical accomplishments. Despite the rumors and scandals that surround him, Jackson will be remembered for his contributions to pop music.

greatest. With production techniques worthy of feature films and high-flying choreography, he transformed videos from static, plotless taped concerts into kinetic, musical dramas that have become integral to the marketing of popular songs.[87]

In addition to being one of the most popular, most successful, and most influential entertainers, Jackson is also one of the most gifted. Although at times it seems that he is known as much for his eccentricities and the rumors, controversies, and scandals that plague him, Michael Jackson is truly a living legend, and in the final analysis he will be remembered for his musical genius and the many contributions he has made.

Notes

Introduction: Entertainer of the '80s

1. Quoted in Michael Jackson, *Moonwalk.* New York: Doubleday, 1988, p. 67.
2. Quoted in J. Randy Taraborrelli, *Michael Jackson: The Magic and the Madness.* New York: Birch Lane Press, 1991, p. 562.

Chapter 1: Born to Perform

3. Quoted in Taraborrelli, *Michael Jackson,* p. 13
4. Quoted in Catherine Dineen, *Michael Jackson: In His Own Words.* London: Omnibus, 1993, p. 43.
5. Quoted in Taraborrelli, *Michael Jackson,* p. 10.
6. Quoted in Taraborrelli, *Michael Jackson,* p. 11.
7. Quoted in Dineen, *Michael Jackson,* p. 54.
8. Quoted in Taraborrelli, *Michael Jackson,* p. 14.
9. Michael Jackson, interview by Oprah Winfrey, American Broadcasting Company, February 10, 1993.
10. Quoted in Lisa D. Campbell, *Michael Jackson: The King of Pop.* Boston: Branden, 1993, p. 196.
11. Quoted in Taraborrelli, *Michael Jackson,* p. 22.
12. Quoted in Taraborrelli, *Michael Jackson,* p. 21.
13. Quoted in Dineen, *Michael Jackson,* p. 10.
14. Quoted in Dineen, *Michael Jackson,* p. 7.
15. Quoted in Dineen, *Michael Jackson,* p. 41.
16. Jackson, interview.
17. Jackson, *Moonwalk,* p. 17.
18. Quoted in Taraborrelli, *Michael Jackson,* p. 18.

19. Quoted in Taraborrelli, *Michael Jackson*, p. 20.

Chapter 2: Michael and Motown

20. Jackson, *Moonwalk*, p. 60.
21. Jackson, *Moonwalk*, p. 67.
22. Jackson, *Moonwalk*, pp. 73, 75.
23. Taraborrelli, *Michael Jackson*, p. 46.
24. Quoted in Taraborrelli, *Michael Jackson*, p. 45.
25. Quoted in Taraborrelli, *Michael Jackson*, p. 66.
26. Jackson, *Moonwalk*, p. 77.
27. Quoted in Taraborrelli, *Michael Jackson*, p. 53.
28. Quoted in Taraborrelli, *Michael Jackson*, p. 54.
29. Quoted in Taraborrelli, *Michael Jackson*, p. 55.
30. Jackson, *Moonwalk*, p. 69.
31. Quoted in Taraborrelli, *Michael Jackson*, p. 43.

Chapter 3: The Down Side of Fame

32. Quoted in Taraborrelli, *Michael Jackson*, p. 70.
33. Quoted in Taraborrelli, *Michael Jackson*, p. 72.
34. Jackson, *Moonwalk*, pp. 90–91
35. Quoted in Taraborrelli, *Michael Jackson*, p. 87.
36. Jackson, *Moonwalk*, p. 90.
37. Quoted in Dineen, *Michael Jackson*, p. 44.
38. Jackson, interview.
39. Jackson, interview.
40. Jackson, interview.
41. Jackson, *Moonwalk*, pp. 95–96.
42. Jackson, *Moonwalk*, p. 96
43. Taraborrelli, *Michael Jackson*, p. 222.

Chapter 4: Breaking Away from Motown

44. Jackson, *Moonwalk*, p. 109.
45. Quoted in Taraborrelli, *Michael Jackson*, p. 113.
46. Quoted in Taraborrelli, *Michael Jackson*, p. 131.
47. Jackson, *Moonwalk*, p. 114.
48. Jackson, interview.
49. Jackson, *Moonwalk*, p. 115.

50. Quoted in Taraborrelli, *Michael Jackson*, p. 153.

51. Jackson, *Moonwalk*, p. 117.

Chapter 5: The Consummate Performer

52. Quoted in Taraborrelli, *Michael Jackson*, p. 160.

53. Jackson, *Moonwalk*, pp. 118, 120.

54. Jackson, *Moonwalk*, p. 123.

55. Quoted in Taraborrelli, *Michael Jackson*, p. 166.

56. Quoted in Taraborrelli, *Michael Jackson*, pp. 204–05.

57. Jackson, *Moonwalk*, pp. 134–35.

58. Jackson, *Moonwalk*, p. 135.

59. Quoted in Taraborrelli, *Michael Jackson*, p. 222.

60. Jackson, *Moonwalk*, p. 138.

61. Quoted in Taraborrelli, *Michael Jackson*, pp. 221–22.

62. Quoted in Taraborrelli, *Michael Jackson*, pp. 230–31.

Chapter 6: Superstardom: The Agony and the Ecstasy

63. Quoted in Dineen, *Michael Jackson*, p. 38.

64. Quoted in Taraborrelli, *Michael Jackson*, p. 257.

65. Quoted in Taraborrelli, *Michael Jackson*, p. 269.

66. Jackson, *Moonwalk*, p. 180.

67. Quoted in Taraborrelli, *Michael Jackson*, p. 309.

68. Quoted in Taraborrelli, *Michael Jackson*, p. 280.

69. Quoted in Taraborrelli, *Michael Jackson*, pp. 281–82.

70. Quoted in Taraborrelli, *Michael Jackson*, p. 174.

71. Jackson, *Moonwalk*, p. 162.

72. Jackson, *Moonwalk*, p. 165.

73. Jackson, *Moonwalk*, p. 166.

74. Taraborrelli, *Michael Jackson*, p. 340.

75. Quoted in Taraborrelli, *Michael Jackson*, p. 344.

76. Jackson, *Moonwalk*, p. 259.

77. Jackson, *Moonwalk*, p. 259.

Chapter 7: The Public Image: Eccentricities and Ridicule

78. Quoted in Taraborrelli, *Michael Jackson*, p. 450.

79. *Jet*, "Michael Jackson Talks About Fame, Plastic Surgery, and 'Thriller,'" December 20, 1999, p. 57.

80. Quoted in Taraborrelli, *Michael Jackson,* p. 433.
81. Quoted in Taraborrelli, *Michael Jackson,* p. 436.
82. Quoted in Taraborrelli, *Michael Jackson,* p. 449.
83. *Jet,* "Michael Jackson Talks About Fame, Plastic Surgery, and 'Thriller,'" p. 57.
84. Jackson, interview.
85. Quoted in Campbell, *Michael Jackson,* p. 71.

Epilogue: Entertainer of the Decade: Accomplishments and Accolades

86. Quoted in Campbell, *Michael Jackson,* p. 274.
87. *Ebony,* "Twenty-Five Who Changed American Music," June 1999, p. 125.

Important Dates in the Life of Michael Jackson

1958
Michael Joseph Jackson is born in Gary, Indiana, on August 29.

1964
The Jacksons enter their first local talent contest.

1965
The Jacksons win their first City-Wide Talent Show.

1967
The Jacksons win the amateur contest at the Apollo Theater.

1968
They are invited back to the Apollo as paid performers; audition for Motown Records.

1969
"I Want You Back," the Jackson Five's first single, reaches number one.

1971
The Jacksons move to their Encino compound.

1974
The Jackson family appears in Las Vegas.

1975
The Jackson Five leave Motown for Epic; Jermaine stays at Motown.

1977
Jackson plays the scarecrow in *The Wiz*.

1979

Off the Wall is released; it becomes CBS Records' biggest-selling album with 12 million sold worldwide.

1982

Thriller is released; becomes the biggest-selling album in history with 51 million sold worldwide.

1983

Jackson appears on "Motown Twenty-Five: Yesterday, Today, and Forever."

1984

Jackson wins eight Grammy Awards.

1985

"We Are the World" record and video are released.

1988

Moonwalk, Jackson's autobiography, is released.

1993

Jackson is charged with child molestation; his interview with Oprah Winfrey is broadcast live from Neverland and is seen by 85 million people worldwide.

1994

Jackson marries Lisa Marie Presley.

1996

Jackson divorces Presley; and marries Deborah Rowe.

1997

Prince Michael Jackson born.

1998

Paris Michael Katherine Jackson is born.

1999

Divorce papers are filed.

For Further Reading

Books

Geoff Brown, *Michael Jackson Body and Soul*. New York: Beauford Books, 1984. This biography gives an insightful portrayal of Jackson's early life and career.

Gordon Matthews, *Michael Jackson*. New York: Wanderer Books, 1984. Written at the height of Jackson's popularity, this book chronicles his rise to fame.

Lois P. Nicholson, *Michael Jackson Entertainer*. New York: Chelsea House, 1984. An overview of Jackson's life and career through the mid-1980s, emphasizing the early years.

Website

Michael Jackson Internet Fan Club (www.mjifc.com). This site is the best resource for information about Jackson. Additionally, it provides links to other related sites.

Works Consulted

Books

Geoff Brown, *The Complete Guide to the Music of Michael Jackson and The Jackson Family*. London: Omnibus, 1996. A track-by-track, album-by-album analysis and guide to the music of Michael Jackson and the Jackson family.

Lisa D. Campbell, *Michael Jackson: The King of Pop*. Boston: Branden, 1993. An overview of Jackson's career, written by an ardent fan.

Catherine Dineen, *Michael Jackson: In His Own Words*. London: Omnibus, 1993. Quotes from and about Jackson.

Michael Jackson, *Moonwalk*. New York: Doubleday, 1988. Jackson's autobiography.

J. Randy Taraborrelli, *Michael Jackson: The Magic and the Madness*. New York: Birch Lane, 1991. An extensively researched and well-documented biography.

Periodicals

Ebony, "Twenty-Five Who Changed American Music," June 1999. An article about twenty-five musicians or singers whose contributions to American music were so large that they took it in new directions. Tells what each artist's contribution was.

Jet, "Michael Jackson Talks About Fame, Plastic Surgery, and 'Thriller,'" December 20, 1999. An article recounting an interview with Michael Jackson that appeared in *TV Guide*.

Interviews

Michael Jackson, interview by Barbara Walters, *20/20*, American Broadcasting Company, September 12, 1997.

———, interview by Oprah Winfrey, American Broadcasting Company, February 10, 1993.

Michael Jackson and Lisa Marie Presley, interview by Diane Sawyer, *Prime Time Live*, American Broadcasting Company, June 14, 1995.

Index

Picture Credits

About the Author

Karen Marie Graves holds a bachelor's degree in English litera-ture and a master's degree in folklore and mythology, specializ-ing in popular culture, from the University of California at Los Angeles. This is her first nonfiction book for young adults. She lives in California with her two children.